What We Believe

Seventh-day
Adventists
Believe

28 True Stories
With Study Guides
for *Guide* Readers

Pacific Press®
Publishing Association
Nampa, Idaho | www.pacificpress.com

Also Edited by Laura Sámano

Mightier Than a Lion

Cover design by Gerald Monks
Cover design resources from Kim Justinen
Inside design by Aaron Troia
Inside illustrations by Mariano Santillan

Copyright © 2020 by Pacific Press® Publishing Association
Printed in the United States of America
All rights reserved

The authors assume full responsibility for the accuracy of all facts and quotations as cited in this book.

Unless otherwise noted, all Scripture quotations are taken from the New King James Version®. Copyright © 1982 by Thomas Nelson. Used by permission. All rights reserved.

Scriptures quoted from CEV are from the Contemporary English Version®. Copyright © 1995 American Bible Society. All rights reserved.

Scripture quotations marked ESV are from The Holy Bible, English Standard Version® (ESV®), copyright © 2001 by Crossway, a publishing ministry of Good News Publishers. Used by permission. All rights reserved.

Scripture quotations marked KJV are from the King James Version.

Scripture quotations marked *The Message* are from *The Message*. Copyright © 1993, 2002, 2018 by Eugene H. Peterson. Used by permission of NavPress Publishing Group.

Scripture quotations marked NIV are from the HOLY BIBLE, NEW INTERNATIONAL VERSION®. Copyright © 1973, 1978, 1984, 2011 by Biblica, Inc.® Used by permission. All rights reserved worldwide.

Scripture quotations marked NLT are from the Holy Bible, New Living Translation, copyright © 1996, 2004, 2007, 2013, 2015 by Tyndale House Foundation. Used by permission of Tyndale House Publishers, Inc., Carol Stream, Illinois 60188. All rights reserved.

Scripture quotations marked NLV are from the New Life Version copyright © 1969 and 2003. Used by permission of Barbour Publishing, Inc., Uhrichsville, Ohio, 44683. All rights reserved.

Additional copies of this book may be purchased by calling toll-free 1-800-765-6955 or visiting AdventistBookCenter .com.

Based on:
Seventh-day Adventists Believe
Copyright © 2018, Third Edition
Ministerial Association
General Conferece of Seventh-day Adventists
12501 Old Columbia Pike
Silver Spring, MD 20904-6600
United States of America
Used by permission

Library of Congress Cataloging-in-Publication Data

Names: Sámano, Laura, editor.
Title: What we believe / Laura Sámano.
Description: Nampa, Idaho : Pacific Press Publishing Association, [2020] |
Audience: Ages 10-14 | Summary: "True stories that correspond with each of the 28 fundamental beliefs of Seventh-day Adventists. A short Bible study is included at the end of each story"— Provided by publisher.
Identifiers: LCCN 2020044865 | ISBN 9780816366781 (paperback) | ISBN 9780816366798 (kindle edition)
Subjects: LCSH: General Conference of Seventh-day Adventists—Doctrines—Juvenile literature.
Classification: LCC BX6154 .W439 2020 | DDC 230/.6732—dc23
LC record available at https://lccn.loc.gov/2020044865

November 2020

Dedication

To my beloved parents, Bernardo and Silvia Sámano, for introducing me to Jesus and showing me His love, and to every person who is searching for a Savior.

Acknowledgments

I start by thanking my family for their never-ending prayers. Lori Futcher, thank you for supporting the concept of this book from the start and for your valuable input. Randy Fishell, Lori Peckham, and Rachel Whitaker Cabose, thank you for mentoring me in the art of editing and for suggesting stories. Randy, thank you for reviewing the Bible study and for writing each of the Faith Seeds. Chantal Klingbeil and the Ellen G. White Estate, I treasure our friendship, and our partnership in ministry is invaluable to me. The stories "Not Ready for Heaven" and "Silencing the Scoffers" originally appeared in the Ellen G. White Estate column in *Guide* and are a courtesy of the estate. Carolyn and Gricelda, thank you for being my right hand in story gathering and author communication.

A special thanks to Karnik Doukmetzian, Jennifer Gray Woods, Alfredo Garcia-Marenko, and Jonas Arrais for facilitating the official 28 fundamental beliefs so that I could include them in this book.

I couldn't make any of you enough banana bread to express my gratitude!

Contents

A special thanks to the authors we were unable to locate. If anyone can provide knowledge of their current mailing address, please relay this information to Laura Sámano, in care of Pacific Press® Publishing Association.

A Word From the *Guide* Editor

A story is told of a man who was asked what he believed. After a short pause, he responded, "Well, I believe what my church believes."

"And what does your church believe?" the man was asked.

The pause was a little longer this time. "Well, my church believes what I believe."

"What do you and your church believe?" the frustrated questioner asked.

"My church and I, well . . . *we're in agreement!*"

Have you ever felt like that man? If someone asked you what you believed, or what your church believes, what would you say?

"Um . . . Saturday church, and dead people don't talk, and something about Jesus' love and heaven, and Ellen White said such and such?"

OK, I'll admit, summarizing what we believe is pretty overwhelming. But the Bible does say we should "always be prepared to give an answer to everyone who asks you to give the reason for the hope that you have" (1 Peter 3:15, NIV).

So I guess you'd better lock yourself in your room until you've memorized our fundamental beliefs. Wait, maybe that's not the best way to learn them. Let's see . . . Jesus was known as a great Teacher, so how did He help people remember overwhelming subjects? Oh yes! Stories!

Ellen White tells us that Jesus "planted in . . . young, expanding minds the seeds of truth that would spring up and produce a plentiful harvest in their riper years."[1]

And that's what we've done here as well. *Guide's* managing editor Laura Sámano has harvested twenty-eight true stories from the pages of *Guide* magazine to introduce each of our beliefs. At the end of each story, you'll find questions to help you dig deeper into each belief.

By the time you're done studying the pages of this book, you might not even want to wait for someone to ask you what you believe before you start sharing with others the fruits of your study.

Lora Fulton

---

1. Ellen G. White, *Child Guidance* (Washington, DC: Review and Herald®, 1954), 265.

Dear Reader

I hope you learn something valuable from each story that I've selected. You'll find a "Faith Seed," a summary of the belief, at the beginning of each story and a Bible study called "Digging in the Word" at the end of each story. By using the verses to answer the questions, you will better understand the biblical foundation of each belief. When you go through the Bible study, you may find it useful to have a journal and a digital Bible handy. I've specified a version of the Bible for some of the questions so that the answers match word for word or for easier understanding. When I don't specify which version, use the New King James Version.

Some chapters' questions include a belief bonus, an interesting fact that might help strengthen your understanding of the belief.

I hope that these stories, questions, verses, and trivia help to deepen your relationship with the Person whom all these beliefs point to, Jesus.

Ask the Holy Spirit to guide you as you read, and I know you'll have a testimony to share!

Laura

Mother's Mysterious Plan

By Isabella Pechaty

🌱 Faith Seed 1: The Holy Scriptures

The Bible is the written word of God.

Marie! Come here!"

Ten-year-old Marie ran quickly to her old house that sat comfortably on a hill. At the door stood Mother, her hair messy and frayed from a busy early morning of work.

"I need you to get me some tomatoes and celery. I can't finish dinner without them." Mother shoved a basket into Marie's hands and rushed back to the messy kitchen to work on supper.

Marie took the basket and began the long journey to the market. She arrived at noon, one of the busiest times for the market. People scurried from stall to stall, hoping to finish last-minute shopping, but something was terribly wrong. The tension in the air was uncomfortably thick.

Marie noticed a somber crowd of people near a wall. Curious, Marie pushed her way to the front of the anxious crowd. The sight that met her eyes was horrible. Pinned to the wall was a large sign that said: "No Bibles allowed—Any Bibles found will be burned."

Marie's knees nearly buckled, and her mouth went dry. For as long as she could remember, a group of cruel men had controlled her country, Czechoslovakia, and many other countries. These men, who called themselves Communists, had formed a government that allowed people no freedom. If one nasty word was said about them, trouble was sure to follow for those who had said it. Marie had heard several stories about the horrible things that the Communists did.

But I never dreamed that they would burn Bibles, thought Marie. Forgetting the tomatoes and celery, Marie dropped the basket and ran toward the safety of home. She found her sisters playing happily in the yard. In spite of their protests, Marie herded her sisters inside and slammed the door.

Marie ran to the kitchen, where her mother waited expectantly for the tomatoes and celery. After taking a deep breath, Marie let out the awful news about the sign in the market. When she finished, her mother sank into a chair and stroked the family Bible lovingly.

"No," she said after a long silence. "The Communists will not find our Bible. Anna, dress Esther for bed. Marie, help Helen bring some flour from the pantry." Everyone rushed out of the room to carry out the instructions. Helen and Marie asked Mother again and again about what her plan was, but Mother's answer was just a triumphant smile.

Before long, Mom sent the girls to bed, but Marie couldn't sleep. She tossed and turned under her quilt until the sounds of cupboards opening and closing stopped, leaving the house quiet and still. Calmed by the sounds of her sisters' quiet conversations, Marie was soon fast asleep.

Wake up! Wake up!" Little Esther was bouncing on Marie's bed, chanting. "Wake up! Wake up!"

Marie groaned and rubbed her sleepy eyes. Then she remembered: The *Communists were coming*! Today! She was out of her bed in seconds. She found everyone in the kitchen, anxiously eating their breakfast. Only Mother seemed calm. She was wiping up spills and washing dishes just as she did every morning.

Marie was eager to learn about her mother's plan for protecting the Bible, but the only thing different that day was some lumpy bread dough rising in the living room.

Marie was puzzled. *Is that Mother's great plan? But how could–?* Her thoughts were cut short by a loud, sharp knocking at the door. Instantly the kitchen flew into action. The girls rinsed their plates, combed their hair one last time, and sat down quietly in their chairs. Marie's palms were sweaty, and her dress itched terribly, but Mother remained calm. She smoothed her hair and walked to the door.

Outside stood a group of five men. The one in the front, a man with an unusually bulbous nose, spoke in a very nasally voice. "By order of the government, we have permission to search your house for any Bibles." He spat out the last word in a disgusted way.

"If you will excuse me, I have something to take care of," replied Mother coldly. She went into the kitchen and placed the bread dough carefully in the oven. "You may begin your search," she said.

The bulbous-nosed officer nodded, and the other four men leaped into action. They overturned pictures on the mantelpiece and searched through the girls' clothes closets. They looked in the cellar and under the beds. They even looked under a loose floorboard. Not a single Bible was found anywhere, but they did smell the delicious aroma of bread baking.

Having found nothing, the four men joined their leader and gave Mother vicious looks. They slammed the door and trudged away. As soon as they left, Mother started laughing. She laughed until tears rolled down her cheeks. When she recovered her composure, she led her four puzzled children to the kitchen, where she took the bread from the oven. All the girls watched as their mother carefully cut the bread in half. When she pulled the golden-brown halves apart, the family Bible was there inside.

This time everyone burst into peals of laughter!

This was not to be the last of the family's troubles, but throughout the rest of their lives, Marie and her sisters had confidence in God. They repeated the scripture that they had heard countless times after the Communists took over:

> Do not fret because of evildoers,
> Nor be envious of the workers of iniquity.
> For they shall soon be cut down like the grass,
> And wither as the green herb (Psalm 37:1, 2).

———————————

Just as mother treasured her Bible, we treasure the Holy Scriptures as God's inspired Word—although we may never have to hide our Bibles from soldiers!

Digging in the Word

1. Who inspired the Bible, and how can it be put into practice each day? 2 Timothy 3:16; Psalm 119:105
2. Where can we find truth? John 17:17
3. How is the Bible described in Hebrews 4:12 and 1 Peter 1:25, NLT?
4. According to 1 Corinthians 10:11, NLT, why was the Bible written?

Camping With the Trinity

By Cathlynn Doré Law

🌱 Faith Seed 2: The Trinity

The Father, Son, and Holy Spirit make up one God.
This three-in-one relationship is called the Trinity.

Callie lugged her sleeping bag and backpack into the cabin as girls excitedly jostled for the best bunks. Spotting an empty bunk in the center of the cabin, she claimed it. Lindy, the girls' teen counselor, was unrolling her sleeping bag onto the bunk across from hers.

"Let's have our heads together so we can whisper when it's time for lights out," Lindy suggested in a conspiratorial undertone. Callie smiled as they arranged their pillows so their heads would be close.

At lunch that day, Callie wasn't the only one famished.

"I think I need five veggie meatballs," Cooper said to the kitchen worker in the serving line.

Smiling knowingly, she said, "You can come back if you want seconds if you're still hungry."

At their cabin that night after campfire, flashlight beams were crisscrossing crazily as girls searched their backpacks to get ready for bed.

"Oh, no!" Mackinsy exclaimed. "I forgot my toothbrush!"

"I did that once," Lindy sympathized.

"What did you do?" Mackinsy moaned.

"I used my finger all week," Lindy said.

"Ewwwwww," a chorus of voices erupted throughout the cabin.

"It was a *clean* finger!" Lindy added quickly, but that probably didn't change anyone's mind.

The next morning a recorded trumpet playing a vigorous "Reveille" jerked every camper awake.

Dear Diary,

I'm going to have to plan better if I'm going to have my personal devotions before the day begins. But better late than never, I suppose!

I've been reading about Jesus' life in the book of John. Elder Roberts, my Bible teacher, says there's no better way to know the God of heaven than by reading His Word every day.

I remember when Elder Roberts told us that. Kyle made a good point. He said, "But I thought no one can see God! So how can we really know Him?"

Elder Roberts reminded us that one of Jesus' disciples asked that same question and had us read about it in John 14:7: "If you had known Me, you would have known My Father also; and from now on you know Him and have seen Him."

That made so much sense to me! We can know God better by learning more about Jesus. That's when I began reading about Jesus' experience on earth. His unselfishness and courage inspire me every day! Tomorrow morning I'll start using my flashlight to read my Bible in the morning.

Following Mr. Kroff through the woods the next day, the group who wanted to earn the flower honor listened as he identified the native blooms he found near camp.

"What are these called?" Terese exclaimed, holding tiny multicolored blossoms between her fingers. "They look like a mini bouquet, don't they?" Callie and Terese picked enough to put in paper cups for the tables in the grub hall.

Callie couldn't decide what her favorite part of campfire was—the songs they sang with nearly bursting lungs or the thoughtful devotional by the camp pastor, Elder Matthews. Tonight Elder Matthews had everyone's attention as he closed his description of Jesus' trial before Pilate.

"Pathfinders, what will you do with Jesus? Will you accept the life He laid down for you and follow Him?" Elder Matthew's tone was serious. "Or will you walk away and do your own thing?"

Dear Diary,

How could anyone walk away and do their own thing? Jesus suffered so much for us!

But as I think about it, I'm remembering last week when Mom had noticed the TV was still warm after she returned home from town. My brother and I had disobeyed her by watching TV when she told us not to.

"It was Doug's idea!" I tried to put the blame on my brother.

With a look of deep disappointment, Mom's eyes held my gaze. "But I told you both to keep the TV off this afternoon."

I am guilty of doing my own thing and trying to blame my brother to excuse my sin of disobedience. I wish I could go home right now to ask Mom's forgiveness!

As Callie pushed noisily into her sleeping bag, her mind was drawn home like a magnet. What were Dad and Mom doing? How was Ginger, her Chihuahua, managing without her? A strange sadness suddenly swept over her. Tears welled up in her eyes. The distance between her and home seemed to grow by the second.

As she sniffed back the persistent tears, she was thankful that everyone in the cabin was asleep. Soft snores and heavy breathing surrounded her. In desperate loneliness, she pulled her arms out from the sleeping bag and draped them limply over her head. Oh, if she could just stop this silly weeping! Trying to relax, she suddenly felt a hand on hers.

It was Lindy! At first, she was embarrassed that someone had heard her. Then her counselor's sympathy brought on fresh tears. Lindy didn't know what she was sad about, but she cared. As Callie's tears subsided, Lindy gave her hand a pat and a squeeze, and gently withdrew hers.

Dear Diary,

I recently read what the Holy Spirit's work is in John 16—guiding, speaking, and convicting of sin. I'm thankful for all these parts of His work. Last night I was especially thankful for the Holy Spirit's other name: Comforter. I'm feeling better now!

The two-day hike down into Waimea Canyon wiped Callie out. She had thought the switchback trail would never come to an end! But the sparkling river running at the bottom of the canyon had been a welcome reward and had refreshed everyone for the return hike back to camp.

That night at campfire, when Elder Matthews ended his devotional, he led the campers in the Lord's Prayer.

"Our Father," he began as usual. Though she had repeated this prayer many times, Callie realized for the first time that Jesus had directed His disciples to pray to God as "our" Father.

Dear Diary,

Is God the Father in a position similar to my father?

On the days Dad is home from work, sometimes he has a list of duties for each family member. Everyone works together on different jobs. It's pretty remarkable how much we accomplish by the end of each day! So maybe God the Father is the one who organizes the Son and the Holy Spirit in the work of saving people.

Last night as we sang "Turn Your Eyes Upon Jesus," I imagined God the Father, God the Son, and God the Holy Spirit bound together in a way I can't really understand and working together on the huge task of saving sinners.

This has certainly been an amazing week camping with the Trinity!

Callie imagined the Trinity working together like a family—God the Father, Jesus, and the Holy Spirit each working at Their own job to fulfill Their united godly purpose.

Digging in the Word

1. When Genesis refers to the creation of a human being, does it refer to God as one or more than one Being? Genesis 1:26, NLT
2. In whose name does Matthew 28:19 say believers are to be baptized?
3. The Three Members of the Godhead were present at what important event in Jesus' life? Luke 3:21, 22

In Line for Disaster

By Ellen Bailey

🫘 Faith Seed 3: The Father

All life and love come from God the Father.

Heream (Her-EEM) finished buckling on her in-line skates and stood up. It was a perfect spring day at Terry Hershey Park in Houston, Texas. Heream's family was going to walk the trails with Pastor and Mrs. Song* and their daughter, Mindy, who was a little bit younger than Heream.

Mindy had brought her bicycle to ride the paved trails. The park was all hills, so both biking and skating were especially good exercise here.

But the perfection of the day was spoiled at the first downhill stretch. Mindy sailed down the slope on her bike, but just as Heream was about to push off to follow, Dad grabbed her hand.

"Dad! I can skate perfectly well by myself," Heream protested.

"Not downhill," Dad said firmly.

"That's right," added Mom. "These hills are steep. You could easily fall and hurt yourself."

"I'll hold your hand going down," said Dad. "That way, I can make sure you don't fall and scrape your knees or even get badly hurt."

"I'm not a baby!" Heream shot back. "I've been in-line skating since I was five! Mindy gets to ride her bike downhill. There's no reason for me to have to hold on like a—a toddler!"

"No ifs, ands, or buts," said Mom. "You hold Dad's hand going downhill."

Heream fumed as she and Dad descended the hill. Of course, she could not go

---

* Some names have been changed to maintain privacy.

18

very fast while being held back this way. And it was the same at the top of each hill. Mindy sped away downhill while Heream held Dad's hand like a baby just learning to walk. It was humiliating!

Too humiliating, she decided as she waited at the top of the next hill. The adults were all absorbed in their conversation, and she was tired of waiting for them to stop talking.

"I'm going down," she announced.

Still talking, his attention on the pastor, Dad held out his hand for Heream to grasp.

"No!" Heream jerked away and shoved off. She rolled smoothly down the paved track, picking up speed.

Oh, yeah! This was what she had come for! The day was warm, and the cool breeze created by her speed felt good on her flushed cheeks. She sped faster and faster. It was like flying! Until . . .

Heream never knew exactly what happened. Just as she reached the bottom of the hill, she suddenly felt herself pitching forward. Desperately she tried to stay upright, flailing her arms and trying to control her feet. But she could not keep her balance.

She smacked into the pavement face-first and kept going. As she slid along the concrete, it felt as if all the skin on her body was being ripped off.

"Heream!" all the adults yelled and came running down the hill. Mindy, halfway up the next hill on her bike, turned back and joined the group around her injured friend.

Heream lay still, too stunned to move for several moments. Her whole body stung like it was on fire. Her knees and elbows felt as if they had been smashed with a hammer. Even her teeth hurt!

Fortunately, Mrs. Song was a nurse. She knelt and examined the injured girl. Blood was streaming from Heream's mouth, where her teeth had cut into her lips.

Mrs. Song wiped at all the bloody places with a handful of tissues and looked carefully at each injury.

"No serious bleeding. That's good."

She pulled out a paper cup and held it under Heream's chin. "Spit." Heream did and was startled to see a chunk of tooth land in the cup. She ran her tongue around her mouth. Oh, no! It was a front tooth that was broken!

"We'll need to get that repaired," observed Mrs. Song. Then she ran her hands over Heream's battered body.

In Line for Disaster

"Can you lift your left arm? Now your right. Your left leg. Right leg." Some more feeling around, a few more pokes and prods, and Mrs. Song sat back on her heels.

"There don't seem to be any broken bones," she told Heream's anxious parents. "Just a lot of very painful scrapes and bruises. Some of those cuts will leave scars, though. When you get home, be sure to bandage the cuts and put ice on the bruises. Some antibiotic cream will soothe the scrapes and keep them from getting infected."

She turned back to Heream. "Do you think you can walk to the parking lot?"

Heream struggled to rise to her feet. "I don't think so," she whispered, and then she toppled sideways. Dad caught her.

"I'll carry you," he said. Lifting his daughter into his arms, he turned back the way they had come.

Dad walked slowly, not wanting to jostle Heream and make her hurt any worse than she already did. Besides, she was not a little girl anymore, and carrying her was hard work. The day was getting warmer every minute, and there were all those hills to climb up! Mom and the Song family followed.

Soon they passed a group of people coming the other way. The curious stares of the strangers were embarrassing. Each time they passed other people, Heream hid her face in her father's shoulder. She felt the sweat there. He was breathing hard too.

"Here, let me carry her for a while," offered Pastor Song.

"Thanks, but I'll do it," said Dad. "I don't want to move her any more than can be helped. She's more comfortable if she stays right where she is."

It was a two-mile walk back to the park entrance and the car. Dad carried Heream every step of the way, without a single complaint. He never even scolded her for her disobedience! His loving kindness made her feel more guilty than ever!

Gently Dad laid her in the back seat of the car. Mom drove home slowly while Dad kept his eyes on his injured child.

The next day as Heream lay in her bed in aching, burning pain, she began to think. She thought of Jesus' story about the shepherd who rescued the lost sheep and carried it home across his shoulders. In much the same way, Dad had carried her so tenderly even though her injuries were her own fault.

It suddenly struck her—that is what God is like! When we are injured and weary, Jesus helps us. He carries us when we cannot walk life's difficult paths. He does not abandon us, even when we're disobedient.

No wonder the Bible says God is love! Heream thought.

Remembering her father's efforts to get her safely back to the car, Heream was filled with thankfulness for the love of Jesus. She knew that He would carry her through until that wonderful day when she and her loving parents would unite with Him in heaven.

Like Heream's father, our Heavenly Father is caring and attentive. He'll pick us up when we fall, but He'd much rather hold our hand so that we don't fall to begin with!

Digging in the Word

1. How does 1 John 4:8 define God?
2. Who exercises authority over everything? 1 Corinthians 15:24–28
3. Who created all things, and how does that shape your view of God? Revelation 4:11

The Waist Gunner's Sacrifice

By Lawrence Maxwell

⌇ Faith Seed 4: The Son

Jesus became human to save us so that
through Him, we can begin again.

One of the bravest men during World War II was a waist gunner on a Flying Fortress. Just ask Sergeant Cunningham.

Cunningham was the radio operator and a gunner on a United States Flying Fortress bomber based at an airfield thirty-five miles north of London.

One day in the spring of 1944, his crew was ordered into the air with a load of bombs for one of the enemy's great cities. Over enemy territory, the air became filled with bursting shells. Through the window, Cunningham saw a plane take a hit in the wing. It began to fall, spinning faster as it went, and two parachutes followed it down. "Two men escaped," Cunningham whispered. "Only two."

He thought of his mom and dad. They were hoping so much he'd come back to them. He looked around the cockpit. Every man there, he knew, had someone who longed for the day he'd be coming home.

Then he glanced down at the fuselage. The waist gunner was bent over his gun, his eyes glued to the window, every muscle tensed, ready to squeeze the trigger the moment an enemy fighter came into range. He was a quiet sort, that waist gunner. Never said very much about himself. But they had talked a few times. And once the gunner had pulled out his wallet and shown him pictures of his kid brother and sister. He was proud of them. "Can't wait to see them again," he had said.

Just then, there was a crackling in the earphones, and Cunningham had to concentrate on a message coming in. But before the message was half finished, there was a tremendous explosion just outside the plane, and a piece of shrapnel pierced the wall and smashed Cunningham's oxygen equipment.

Cunningham knew that he was doomed. In minutes he would pass out, and then, unconscious and helpless, he would die from lack of oxygen at that high altitude. Already he was growing dizzy. He fumbled with the valves. He was falling . . .

Gift of Life

Moments later, Sergeant Cunningham opened his eyes. What had happened? His head ached. Why was he on the floor? What was that hole in the fuselage? Oh, yes, a shell—it had broken his oxygen mask. Then what was this mask on his face? Why was he still able to breathe?

He struggled to get up and look around.

Just a few feet away, his face to the floor, lay the waist gunner. Dead. His oxygen mask was gone.

Sergeant Cunningham was wearing it! The waist gunner had put it on him, then died in his place.

"Greater love has no one than this, than to lay down one's life for his friends" (John 15:13).

Jesus said that years ago, and the waist gunner followed His example.

The waist gunner knew what it was like to consider others as better than himself (Philippians 2:3) and offer the greatest sacrifice (John 15:13). Jesus sacrificed His own life so that we could live forever.

Digging in the Word

1. How does the Bible describe Jesus' nature? Mark 10:45; 1 John 5:20; Hebrews 4:15
2. What did Jesus accomplish when He came to the earth? 1 Corinthians 15:3, 4
3. What characteristic of Jesus does Paul say we need to adopt? Philippians 2:3-7, NLV

Warrior With a Difference

By Norma Trood

◷ Faith Seed 5: The Holy Spirit

The Holy Spirit inspires us, gives us spiritual power,
and guides our understanding.

Fear gripped Korima as his young feet pounded the rough jungle track. His eyes were wide, and sweat ran down his dusky face. When he burst into the village clearing, his voice rang with alarm.

"Mama, Mama, I don't want to be a spirit man."

Serapta quickly stood up from the grass mat she was weaving and watched with anxious eyes as her sturdy young son ran toward her.

"Korima, who said you were going to be a spirit man?" she asked.

"Wooru said so. But I don't want to be a spirit man. I want to be a brave warrior."

"What did Wooru say that makes you think you are to be a spirit man?"

"Mama, I was going through the village to the dispensary to get the medicine for Grandmother. I had to go past the church house where the people in Wooru's village meet. Lots of people were in the church house. Wooru was speaking, and I heard him say, 'May Korima be filled with Your spirit.' "

"That is a strange thing for Wooru to say." Serapta looked sharply at her son. "So you did not get the medicine for Grandmother?"

Korima hung his head. "No, Mama."

"Korima, Grandmother is very ill. Go back to the village and bring medicine from Wooru."

"I am afraid, Mama. Wooru wants me to have an evil spirit. I am frightened of evil spirits."

"Wooru is a good man. You know he does not have evil spirits. He is not a spirit man. He is a nurse boy and helps those who are sick. You do not need to be afraid."

What We Believe

Serapta put her arm around her son's shoulder and began to walk toward the jungle track with him. "Go quickly, Korima. Grandmother needs the medicine."

"Mama, must I go?" Korima looked pleadingly at his mother.

"Please go. Don't you want to be a brave warrior?"

Korima sighed, then stood straight as he replied, "Yes, Mama, I will run fast."

Once more Korima ran through the jungle track to the village where Wooru lived. He ran past the fine church house with bright flowers blooming around it. He hurried past the village homes with their neat gardens—so different from his village. Korima went quickly to the dispensary nestled among shady coconut palms. His hand shook as he knocked against the woven wall.

"Ah, Korima, my friend, it is good to see you!" A friendly smile lit Wooru's shiny black face as he came to the door. "What brings you to this village today?"

"Grandmother needs medicine." Korima looked at the ground as he spoke.

"How is Grandmother?" Wooru asked.

"Very sick," Korima replied.

"Korima, would you wait a few minutes while I finish attending a patient? Then I will come with you to see your grandmother."

A little later, as Korima and Wooru followed the path back to Korima's village, Wooru said, "I have not seen you for a while. Where have you been?"

"I came earlier today. You were in the church house."

"You could have come into the church house with the other people and listened to the stories I told."

Korima squirmed uncomfortably. "I did not want to."

"Oh, why not? You seem to enjoy listening to the stories I tell about Jesus."

Korima's voice was husky as he replied, "I heard you say you wanted me to be a spirit man."

Wooru's long strides stopped suddenly as he swung around to face Korima. "When did I say I wanted you to be a spirit man?"

"Today, when you were in the church house. I had come for medicine for Grandmother, but you were in the church house with many other people. And I heard you say, 'May Korima be filled with Your spirit.' I didn't want to be a spirit man, so I ran home quickly. Wooru, I don't want to be a spirit man. I want to be a warrior." The words tumbled out of Korima.

A wide grin spread across Wooru's face, and his brown eyes twinkled. "My young friend, I think you do not understand what I meant when I said those words. Come, we will go to see your grandmother. Then you and I will go and sit by the stream at your village while I tell you what I meant. Let me assure you, Korima, I do not want you to be a spirit man."

When Wooru arrived at Korima's house, he spoke kindly to Serapta and visited with Grandmother, leaving medicine for her.

Then he and Korima went to the stream and sat on sun-drenched stones while water splashed around their feet. Wooru began, "Korima, today in the church I was praying to Jesus, who died for us. When He rose from the dead, He went back to heaven. He sent His Holy Spirit to help us so we can be like Him. The Holy Spirit comes into our lives to help us think good thoughts and do the right things. This is what we mean by being filled the Holy Spirit. So today I asked the Holy Spirit to come into your life and fill you so that you would become like Jesus. That is when you heard me say, 'May Korima be filled with Your Spirit.' "

"Oh, is that what you meant?" Korima looked thoughtful as he watched the water ripple and sparkle in the late-afternoon sun. "You don't want me to be a spirit man? You don't want me to have a bad spirit? You want me to have a good spirit?"

"I want you to have the Holy Spirit dwelling in you," Wooru said firmly.

"Do you have the Holy Spirit dwelling in you?" Korima asked earnestly.

"Yes, Korima. Every day I ask to be filled with the Holy Spirit."

Korima didn't understand. "You ask for the Holy Spirit, yet you are not a spirit man?"

"Not the way you understand spirit man. I love Jesus, and I want to be filled with His Holy Spirit. I know I am free from evil spirits because the Holy Spirit has great power."

"More power than a bad spirit man?"

"Yes, much more power than any bad spirit man."

"And the Holy Spirit will help me?" Korima asked.

"Yes."

"And the Holy Spirit will keep me from the bad spirits?"

"Yes."

Korima jumped up. What he had just heard made his eyes sparkle like the sunlit water at his feet. "Wooru, I must go and tell Mama!"

"We will talk more about Jesus and the Holy Spirit!" Wooru called as Korima ran to his house.

Over the weeks and months, Korima learned many, many things about Jesus. When he talked with Wooru, he went back to Serapta and excitedly told her what he had learned. The life of Jesus and the Holy Spirit filled his life, just as Wooru had promised.

Korima was determined to go to school so that he could help his people. He wanted to be like Wooru and help them when they were sick. He wanted to teach them more of Jesus. He wanted to help them clean up their villages and build new houses with gardens around them, churches with shrubs and flowers around them, dispensaries with trees and green grass around them, and schools with playgrounds around them.

Korima's big feet sped along the rough jungle track. His eyes sparkled, and a broad grin crossed his face. When he burst into the village clearing, his voice rang with excitement. "Mama, Mama, I am home at last!"

Serapta slowly stood up from the grass mat she was weaving and watched with age-dimmed eyes as the strong figure of her grown son ran toward her.

"Mama, I want to be a man full of the Holy Spirit." They both laughed as they thought of the day long ago when Korima ran to her, afraid he had to be a bad spirit man when instead he wanted to be a warrior. "Oh, my son, it is wonderful to have you back! Tell me about the many years you have been away."

"When I left here and went to the mission school, I soon realized how much education I really needed. I finished primary school there and went away to another island to a high school. When I finished there, I went to yet another island to college, where I studied to be a minister. I also learned how to grow better gardens, to build stronger homes, and to bring water into the village. I learned first aid and all about keeping well and strong. Now that I have graduated from college, I have been appointed to be the minister for this valley and to take the story of Jesus to all the surrounding area!"

Korima stood straight and tall. When he spoke, his face shone with conviction. "Mama, I am a warrior at last. But I am not a warrior with bows and arrows to defend this village. I am a warrior with a difference. I am a warrior filled with the Holy Spirit to defend the truth of the Lord Jesus Christ!"

You don't need to become a "spirit man" or "spirit woman" to be filled with God's Holy Spirit. Like Korima and Wooru, you can invite the Holy Spirit to fill your heart every day.

Digging in the Word

1. Who did Jesus say would be with believers after He went back to heaven? John 14:16-18
2. What does the Holy Spirit do? John 14:25, 26
3. What else did Jesus promise the Helper (Holy Spirit) would do when He came? John 16:7, 8
4. What did Jesus promise would happen when the Holy Spirit came upon them? Acts 1:8
5. What does the Holy Spirit do for people who pray? Romans 8:26, NLT

Why Geese Fly Farther Than Eagles

By Crystal Earnhardt

🗂 Faith Seed 6: Creation
God created all things in nature,
and humans are to enjoy and care for them.

Jesse fidgeted as Mr. Hess droned on, his voice sounding as monotonous as a buzzing mosquito. Science just didn't interest him, and this teacher was as dry as the desert sand.

I need to improve my grade. He yawned. *I've got to focus.* He stretched his arms out and shook them slightly.

Sara, who sat beside him, raised her hand. "So what you're saying is that all forms of life came from one thing even if they were designed totally different—such as a whale and an oak tree?"

"Evolved totally different," the teacher corrected her. "We are all distant cousins. The central idea of biological evolution is that all life on earth shares a common ancestor, just as you and your cousins share a common grandmother. Whales and hummingbirds, tigers and giraffes. Animals change over time in order to survive. A fish needed to develop gills because it needed to be able to breathe underwater."

"I have a hard time applying that to fish who have two eyes, and then knowing about the four-eyed fish," Sara commented.

Mr. Hess looked confused. "What do you mean, Sara?" he asked.

"There is a fish called the four-eyed fish," Sara explained. "It appears to have four eyes, but in reality, its pupils are split into two parts. One part is on top looking up, and the other part is facing underwater. The fish can see danger from above and underneath. My dad says that it is one of a kind. That same fish lives in the same environment as other fish. This didn't happen in order to adapt. There is no other fish like that to evolve from. My dad says that God created each animal unique."

Why Geese Fly Farther Than Eagles

"I understand that many of you are taught differently at home," the teacher said. "But here at school, you are graded by what you know from this textbook, not by what your parents believe." He looked around to emphasize his point. "Do you understand? Class is dismissed."

"Wow, Sara!" Jesse exclaimed as they gathered up their books. "Where did your dad learn about the four-eyed fish?"

"He saw it in Mexico," Sara replied, "but he believes that God created everything. How else would you explain a woodpecker?"

Just then, Jesse's cell phone buzzed. He glanced at the screen and turned off the reminder that history class was beginning in five minutes. Sara was far more interesting. "Sorry for the interruption," he said. "Are you talking about the redheaded bird that hammers into trees to eat?"

"That's it." Sara grinned. "It pecks and pulls out insect larva at speeds up to sixteen miles per hour. Any other bird would break its neck just banging its head on a window, but the woodpecker has a cushion around its head like a helmet. Do you understand what I'm saying? Nature and humans are too complex to evolve from nothing. That same bird has a tube that circles its head and brain to store its extra-long tongue." She pointed to his cell phone. "It's like saying that pieces of metal just came together and formed a phone with all the information included."

Jesse shook his head. "You've got a point. I don't know what to believe, but I'll think about it this weekend."

That night at the supper table, Jesse shared some of the conversation with his parents. Mom just shook her head.

"Better listen to your teacher and bring your grades up," Dad grunted.

"Want to go camping down by the lake this weekend?" Grandpa interrupted. "The geese should be leaving soon."

Jesse sighed. Clearly, no one in his family knew anything about evolution or creation. Going to the lake might be a good way to clear his head and think it over.

The next day he and Grandpa pitched their tent on a grassy knoll overlooking the lake. Warm, gentle sunshine promised good weather. They hiked and fished and watched the geese.

Grandpa didn't say much until late afternoon, when the geese seemed of one accord to just pick up, circle the lake, and soar off in a perfect V formation.

"Did you know that geese can fly farther than eagles can?" Grandpa asked.

"How come?" Jesse asked. "Eagles are bigger and stronger."

"The geese have a secret."

"What is it, Grandpa?"

"When they migrate on long trips, they don't fly alone. You see that one at the tip of the V? Its outstretched neck is like a spear slicing the wind or breaking the air. That causes an upward wind that lifts the birds behind it. The others don't have to flap so hard. They're kind of riding on a draft. When the lead bird gets tired, it simply drops back, and another bird takes the lead."

"That's so cool," Jesse commented thoughtfully. "And how did they learn that?"

"That's called instinct," Grandpa answered as he picked a blade of grass and chewed on it. "They know when to fly south for the winter, and they mate for life. A goose will show sorrow over a fallen mate. Now tell me, Son, how does instinct evolve? How do birds just know this stuff?"

Jesse nodded his head. "I understand now what Sara was saying." He looked at his phone. "There are some things that are just too complex to evolve. If that's the case, then that would mean there is a Creator!"

"Now you're getting it." Grandpa chuckled.

———————————

Jesse could see evidence of the Creator's work in the natural world around him. The Bible confirms that the world we live in didn't just happen by accident!

Digging in the Word

1. Who created planet Earth? Genesis 1:1
2. How long did the process take? Genesis 1:3-31
3. Whom did God make according to His image? Genesis 1:27, NLT

The Most Valuable Treasure

By Charles Mills

🍃 Faith Seed 7: The Nature of Humanity

Humans are born with a sinful nature,
but by God's grace, we can live above "sin level."

Philip sighted down the long steel barrel of his gun, waiting for just the right moment to pull the trigger. His target was Martino, who stood partially exposed in the crowded Rio de Janeiro market, shopping for groceries and totally unaware that his life could end violently at any moment.

He deserves to die, Philip thought, a hint of a smile creasing his otherwise serious face. *He stole my most valuable possession. He snuck into my home and took my precious gem—a jewel I'd spent years working hard to purchase. In one moment, it was gone, and this man, this creature, this worthless thief, has taken it from me.*

A trickle of sweat ran along the eyebrow above Philip's sighting eye and moved down his cheek as his thoughts continued. *The police are doing nothing. Nothing! But I will do something. I will get my revenge.*

The man's finger moved ever so slightly, increasing the pressure on the weapon's trigger. Then it stopped. *Why?* Philip thought. *Why can't I do this?*

Martino moved in among the crowd, and the opportunity for a clean, unobstructed shot vanished. Philip's shoulders sagged as he pointed the barrel of his gun skyward. *Maybe this isn't the best time for this,* he reasoned. *I'll try again soon.*

Days passed. The anger seething in Philip's mind intensified until once again he stood, unseen, with his gun leveled at his self-proclaimed enemy. But, as before, he couldn't pull the trigger. What was wrong? Martino had done a terrible thing, a selfish thing, a life-changing thing to him. He'd robbed Philip not only of his gem but also his whole future. Philip had spent all of his savings to buy that gem. Now both the gem and his life savings were gone. Martino had taken them both.

The Most Valuable Treasure

One afternoon, about three months later, Philip was passing a church on his way home from the market and thought, *Maybe I ought to go to services before I kill Martino. After all, God is a vengeful god. He'll understand my need to destroy the man who destroyed my life.* He nodded thoughtfully as the idea took root in his mind. *Yes. That's what I'll do. I'll attend services. I'll let God motivate me into action. I'm sure that's what the preacher will tell me—that I can take my revenge with God's blessing. I won't hesitate next time I have the opportunity to end Martino's life.*

But that day, the pastor's sermon wasn't about revenge. As Philip sat in his seat near the back of the church, he heard a very different message.

"When Jesus confronted sinners," the pastor declared from behind his tall, wooden pulpit, "He didn't bring condemnation and revenge on them—things they fully deserved. He did something unexpected, something unusual, something even more powerful than justice. He forgave them. He called them 'blessed.' He told them to stop doing evil and to start doing good. That was His message of revenge. That was His judgment on sinners."

What! Philip gasped inwardly. *That's not right. God is a god of rage, of punishment, of hellfire and destruction. I've never heard this kind of message before.*

"You see," the preacher continued, "during the centuries after Adam and Eve walked the beautiful paths of the Garden of Eden, human beings had developed a wrong image of God. They'd become afraid of Him. They'd stopped trusting in Him. They thought He was full of rage and anger. That's one of the reasons Jesus had come to earth: to show everyone what God the Father is really like. Jesus said in John fourteen, verse nine, 'Anyone who has seen me has seen the Father' [NIV]. Then He stated in John ten, verse thirty, 'I and the Father are one' [NIV].

"So if you want to know how to act like God, spend time learning about Jesus. He was God on earth. His message was love, not hate, salvation, not revenge."

Then it seemed that the preacher looked directly at Philip. "The nature of humanity—our nature—is sinful," he said softly. "It's easy for us to hate others and to want them to pay for their sins. But the nature of God is love. He wants to save us from our sins, to bring us into His family so that we can live forever with Him in heaven. That's the way we should treat others, even those who have done evil things to us."

That evening, Philip sat alone in his house, holding the gun in his hand. He studied the contours of the weapon and felt its smoothness against his fingers. Then he stood, moved across the room, and placed the weapon in the big, sturdy safe resting against the wall.

With stars twinkling overhead, he walked to the church where he'd attended services earlier that day. He found the preacher inside straightening the songbooks in the chairs. "I want you to know something, Pastor," he said with tears in his eyes. "Today I decided that, instead of taking a man's life, I'm going to start a new life in Jesus."

The man smiled broadly, extending his hand. "Tell me your story," he invited.

The two men sat together as Philip shared his sad saga about how something valuable had been taken from him and how he wanted the thief to pay with his life. About how, twice, he couldn't carry out his revenge. Then he came to church and learned about the true God of love.

The preacher nodded and smiled warmly. "Seems God is already working on your heart," he said. "Instead of taking a man's life, you've started a new life in Christ. That's the most valuable treasure of all."

Ever since Eve fell for the serpent's temptation, all people—Philip, you, and even Martino—have what is called a "fallen nature." Without God's all-powerful help, we cannot be good.

Digging in the Word

1. What did God say would happen to Adam and Eve if they disobeyed Him? Genesis 2:17
2. How does King David describe himself at birth? Psalm 51:5, NLT
3. Humanity has what kind of heart? Jeremiah 17:9
4. What hopeful message does 2 Corinthians 5:18 provide?
5. God created us for His glory (Isaiah 43:7). What does He ask Christians to do? Mark 12:29-31; Numbers 35:33, 34

Light to Defeat Darkness

By Rachel Whitaker Cabose

🖋 Faith Seed 8: The Great Controversy

An unseen spiritual battle is taking place between God's good forces and Satan's evil army. Each side hopes to win your loyalty.

A trace of winter's chill hung in the March air as carriages and wagons drove up to the small schoolhouse. The year was 1858 in Lovett's Grove, a quaint town in rural Ohio.

The people crowding into the building were dressed in black. The somber faces reflected the occasion: the funeral of a young man who was dear to many of them.

But despite the sad event, there was an undercurrent of excitement in the room. A special speaker was to give the funeral sermon—James White, a well-known preacher from Michigan. James and his wife, Ellen, were visiting for the weekend, and many in the audience had come more to hear him than to pay their respects to the deceased man.

Only a few weeks before, there had been no believers in Lovett's Grove who kept Saturday as their day of worship. But an Adventist evangelist had been holding meetings in the schoolhouse, and forty people had accepted the Bible truth of the seventh-day Sabbath. It was an honor to receive a visit so soon from the movement's best-known leaders—James and Ellen White.

Boots scuffed against the rough board floor as people squeezed closer together in their seats. Some had to stand outside—the schoolhouse was full!

The low voices hushed when James stood to speak. He preached a moving sermon.

Then Ellen rose to her feet. "I feel urged by the Spirit to share my thoughts with you as well," she said. The crowd settled back in their seats, eager to hear what she had to say.

Ellen's face glowed with enthusiasm as she spoke of Jesus' second coming. "Those who have died believing in Jesus will be raised to life again. There will be no more death, no more sorrow and weeping such as we experience here today. What a wonderful hope we have as Christians!"

Suddenly Ellen paused in her talk. "Glory to God!" she called out. "Glory to God!"

James stepped quickly toward his wife, who was gazing into the distance. "My wife is having a vision," he explained to the audience. "God often gives her special messages to encourage and guide His people, just as He spoke to the prophets in Bible times."

The people were surprised to see that while Ellen was in vision, she did not breathe, but she could still walk around. At times she even spoke a few words, evidently reacting to the scenes she was seeing.

For two hours, the crowded schoolhouse was quiet as the people watched Ellen throughout her vision. The funeral was almost forgotten.

Finally, she began to breathe again and to notice the people around her. Realizing that the vision had ended, the family and close friends of the young man who had died left to take the casket to the cemetery. But many people stayed behind, hoping to hear what Ellen had seen in the vision.

They were not disappointed. God had given Ellen special counsels for the believers in Lovett's Grove. There were words of encouragement for some who had chosen to follow God's truth even though their family had not. There were messages of instruction for those who needed to use their money to help God's work.

"But God showed me so much more than this," Ellen said. "He showed me the whole story of this world from beginning to end, starting with Satan's fall even before this earth was created. I saw God's plan for getting rid of sin forever. He wants us to know these things because we are living at the very end of time."

Ellen's listeners leaned forward, wanting to hear more. "I can't even begin to tell all the details right now," she said. "But God has told me that I should write down what I have seen so that everyone can read it."

The people filed out of the schoolhouse to return to their homes and farms, thoughtful as they looked back over the remarkable events of the day. What a privilege to hear God's messages especially for them!

Ellen smiled up at her husband as the carriage jounced along the road toward Fremont, Ohio. "Just think—in two days we'll be home in Battle Creek," Ellen said. "I can't wait to see Henry, Edson, and Willie again!"

James patted his young wife's hand. "I know you miss our boys when we have to travel. Especially little Willie. But doing God's work requires us to sacrifice."

"I know," Ellen said. She gazed at the leafless trees along the road, remembering something from her vision the day before. "You will have to contend with the powers of darkness," the angel had told her. "Satan will make strong efforts to hinder you from writing out this message. But keep trusting in God. Angels will be with you in the conflict."

What new difficulties lie ahead for us? Ellen wondered.

The next morning James and Ellen eagerly boarded the train for Jackson, Michigan. As the train rocked and swayed through the countryside, Ellen and James pulled out their writing instruments and began to work. When they traveled, James usually had articles to complete for the *Advent Review and Sabbath Herald** magazine he published, and Ellen often wrote letters containing the counsels God had shown her in vision.

"As soon as we get home, I'm going to start writing about what I saw in the vision this weekend," Ellen spoke up. "The information is very important for the church. God has shown me some of it before, but this time, I saw the whole picture so clearly. All through the ages, God has been doing everything He can to save us, but Satan has been trying his best to turn us against God and bring us to eternal death along with him."

"Maybe you can write an article in an upcoming *Review*," James suggested.

"No, there's far too much material for that! I will need to write an entire book," Ellen said. "I'd like to call it *The Great Controversy Between Christ and His Angels and Satan and His Angels*. People must know about the battle for their loyalty that is going on behind the scenes."

"Hmmm," James mused, listening for a moment to the rhythmic *clickety-clack* of the train wheels. "That book title sounds a lot like the title of a book we read earlier this year."

"Yes, but that author had it all wrong!" Ellen exclaimed, her eyes sparkling with passion as she warmed to her subject. "He called his book *The Great Controversy Between God and Man*. God is not fighting against us. He's on our side! This book will show that the real fight is between God and the forces of evil."

"And God will win in the end," James said with a smile.

"Of course! In fact, Jesus has already won the victory," Ellen replied. She settled her head against the seat back for a short rest.

---

* This magazine is now known as the *Adventist Review*.

What We Believe

When the train arrived in Jackson, Ellen and James hurried to the home of Dan and Abigail Palmer, glad for the chance to rest and visit with friends before continuing their trip. The Palmers had been the first Sabbath-keeping Adventists in Michigan, and they were always happy to host the Whites in their home.

Soon Ellen and Abigail were carrying on a lively conversation. Ellen told of the meetings she and James had held in Ohio. "We had so many blessings on our trip!" she exclaimed. "In Lovett's Grove, we met with forty new Sabbathkeepers. And to think there were none in that town just a few weeks ago."

"Wonderful!" agreed Abigail. "How did the group grow so fast?"

Ellen opened her mouth to reply, but she couldn't say a word. Her tongue felt swollen and numb. A strange cold sensation struck her heart and then surged through her head and down her right side. She caught Abigail's look of surprise and concern, and then she fell unconscious against her chair.

"Dan! James! Come quickly! Something has happened to Ellen!" Abigail called.

The three gathered around Ellen's unconscious form. "We must pray for God to heal her," James said. As they earnestly pleaded with God to restore her to health, Ellen's eyes fluttered open.

"Ellen, how do you feel?" James asked anxiously. "Can you move your arms and legs?"

Ellen slowly wiggled her right hand and foot, but she couldn't move her left side at all.

"She's had strokes of paralysis like this before," James explained to the Palmers. "We can only pray that this one will go away as the others did."

Ellen feebly reached for her husband's hand. "James," she whispered hoarsely, "I don't know if I'm going to make it this time. Tell the children how much I love them."

"But Ellen," James protested, "you must hang on. We're less than fifty miles from home. God still has work for you to do. I'm sure of it."

They all bowed in prayer again. Soon Ellen's face brightened. "I can feel a prickling sensation in my left arm and leg. I can even move them a little. Praise God!"

The next morning Ellen felt strong enough to continue the trip. But when they reached home in Battle Creek, she was too exhausted to walk up the steps of their house. James tenderly carried her up the steep stairs to the second-floor bedroom.

For the next few weeks, Ellen felt weak and numb. When she tried to walk, she had trouble keeping her balance and sometimes fell to the floor. But her illness did not cloud her mind.

"I must start writing what I saw in the vision," she said one morning shortly after they had arrived home. She was barely strong enough to sit up. But there in the upstairs bedroom, pen in hand, she slowly and painfully wrote a few words at a time.

"The Lord has shown me that Satan was once an honored angel in heaven, next to Jesus Christ," she began. She laid down her pen to rest for a few minutes as the scenes from the vision played through her mind.

Ellen wrote about how Satan became jealous of Jesus and wanted to have the highest place in heaven. Finally, she finished one page. Exhausted, she lay back down in bed.

It took three days before she felt well enough to continue. But again, she could write only one page. "At this rate, I may never finish the book," she said to James.

But as she kept working, her strength increased, and eventually, she was back to full health. God showed her in vision that her attack of illness had been a direct attempt by Satan to take her life. But just as God had promised, angels had come to rescue her from the enemy's power.

By May, Ellen was well enough to speak at a meeting of four hundred believers in Battle Creek. There she told some of the things God had shown her in the vision.

Tears came to many eyes as she described the suffering and death of Jesus. "The angels could hardly bear to watch the horrible scene," she told her audience. "They wanted to rescue Jesus from the men who were insulting and abusing Him. Jesus knew that the weakest angel in heaven could cause the whole multitude to fall powerless. But instead of asking God to deliver Him, He chose to go through with the plan for our salvation."

As always, Ellen's goal was to turn hearts toward the Savior.

Through the summer, Ellen wrote on, and God's Holy Spirit guided her as she worked. She told about great Christians such as Martin Luther and William Miller and the ways God had used them to point people to His truth. She told about the deceptions Satan uses to distract people from following God. And then she looked ahead to the time when Jesus would come again to take His faithful followers home to heaven.

Ellen pictured again the beauty of the New Jerusalem, the throne of God, and the tree of life. She especially remembered the loving look on Jesus' face as He welcomed His people to their new home.

Finally, she had to lay down her pen in amazement. "O what love!" she exclaimed out loud. "What wondrous love! The most exalted language cannot describe the glory of heaven, nor the matchless depths of a Savior's love."

One evening in August, Ellen met James at the door when he came home from the Review and Herald Publishing Association office. "The book is finished," she announced happily. "And the ending is my favorite part."

"Let's hear it," James said. He sat down and closed his eyes as Ellen turned to the last page of her manuscript. The final paragraph described what she had seen of the new earth.

"God's entire universe was clean, and the great controversy was forever ended," Ellen began. "Everywhere we looked, everything the eye rested upon was beautiful and holy."

She read down to the end of the page. Then she looked up at her husband.

"We'll be with Jesus forever and ever," Ellen murmured. "And that's the best part of the whole story."

We are still living in the middle of the great controversy that Ellen White saw in vision and wrote about, but it will soon be over when Jesus comes to rescue us.

Digging in the Word

1. Who introduced sin to the earth? Genesis 3:1; Revelation 12:9
2. Where did the conflict between Lucifer and God begin? Isaiah 14:12–14
3. Who is watching the great conflict? 1 Corinthians 4:9
4. What is the result of a sinful life? What does Christ offer us? Romans 6:23
5. What does God give to guide, protect, and sustain you in the way of salvation? John 16:7-9; Hebrews 1:14, NLT

The Story No One Wanted to Miss

By Cathlynn Doré Law

Faith Seed 9: The Life, Death, and Resurrection of Christ

Jesus came to free us from being held hostage to sin.
When we accept His sacrifice, we claim eternal life.

Boom! Boom! Boom! The missionaries sat beside the blazing campfire watching the gyrating, masked village men dance to the monotone beat of the drums.

"The men wearing the masks are supposed to be dead ancestors," an elder explained. "When I was a boy, my mother saw the mask in our hut. She then *knew* that it was my dad who wore it." Overcome by sudden emotion, the man looked down. When he could continue, he said, "Mother was taken into the jungle and strangled because she had seen the mask."

The missionaries began to understand the constant fear the villagers lived with. It was time for the people in this isolated village of New Guinea to hear about Jesus!

The missionary invited the native people to a meeting. Sensing something important was about to be shared, the whole village came—310 adults and children. The missionary lifted an open Bible. "This God-talk [the Bible] has been given so you can know the truth. Let me tell you of the God who sent this Bible to you. God is kind. He is love. He is forgiving," the missionary described.

As the stories from the Old Testament began to unfold Monday through Friday, twice a day, the villagers didn't want to miss one! Sometimes the sick were brought on their mats. One time a mother about to give birth was positioned close to the gathering so she could listen. Midway through the Bible story, the cries of the newborn were heard!

Beginning at Genesis, the Creation story was told—and then Adam and Eve's tragic choice to sin. When God promised to send His Son as a Savior, the missionary held a stuffed white lamb and explained the sacrificial service, which illustrated how God's beloved Son would finally die for humanity's sins.

"I need some volunteers," the missionary said one day. He had found that acting out the story was very effective. When he began to tell the story of Abraham and Isaac, a hush fell over the listeners as the missionary described the agony of father Abraham as he wrestled with the command he had been given. The God whom Abraham loved had asked him to kill the son he loved as a sacrifice. At this climax in the story, the missionary dismissed the villagers. Many struggled to figure out what would happen. *What would Abraham do?*

Early the next day, the missionary had a visitor. The visitor's bloodshot eyes showed that he had missed hours of sleep the night before. He got right to the point.

"Abraham, he love God. Abraham, he love his son." The troubled man shook his head. Then meeting the missionary's eyes, he declared, "Abraham, he obey God." Then raising his finger toward heaven, he predicted, "God, He get another lamb!"

Amazed at the man's insight, the missionary patted the visitor's shoulder. "You come to the meeting this morning. You will hear what Abraham will do. You will hear what God will do."

Before the meeting, three other men came separately to the missionary with the same conclusion.

During the story that day, the dilemma was resolved. The angel stopped Abraham from plunging the knife into his son's heart. Then Abraham found the ram caught in the bushes and offered it as a substitute sacrifice for Isaac, his son.

As the story continued, the missionary told of Sodom and Gomorrah being destroyed because of their sin. Recognizing their own sin, the villagers said, "We are just like those people in Sodom and Gomorrah."

For two months, the missionary shared Old Testament stories that showed God's greatness and His grace in providing the lamb sacrificial service to atone for humanity's sinful, lost condition.

One day the missionary said, "It was time for God to send His Son. He sent Him as a tiny baby. His name was Jesus."

Baby Jesus grew to be a boy and then a young man. The magnificent stories of the New Testament opened the villagers' hearts to Jesus—this God-man who had time for little children, the Teacher who sat on the hillside and explained God's truth, the Son of God who ate with sinners, the Miracle Man who cast out demons and multiplied food, the Healer who opened blind eyes and even raised dead Lazarus. This wonderful Jesus could do anything. He became their hero. With every story, they loved Him more.

So intense was the people's interest in the story of Jesus, they forgot to eat at mealtimes. After the story ended each evening, they lingered—discussing the story and ignoring normal sleep time.

Early one morning as sunrise painted the dark sky, the eager listeners gathered. The missionary began to tell the story of Judas's betrayal. Appalled, the people watched the reenactment of men roughly tying Jesus' hands and leading Him away to the judgment hall. With unbelieving eyes and ears, they heard Pilate's admission that Jesus was innocent of any sin, and watched as Pilate gave Jesus over for execution. Heads bowed as actor-soldiers began beating their precious Jesus. Finally, hands covered unwilling eyes that could not watch as Jesus was tied to the cross and lifted up to hang, helpless and limp.

Somber faces followed the friends to the tomb where they laid Jesus' dead body. Tears fell at this final end of their dear Jesus.

But the story turned a dramatic corner when Jesus' friends discovered the tomb to be empty after a mournful, dark night! Listeners were as puzzled as Jesus' friends had once been. When His friend Mary Magdalene recognized Jesus' voice in the garden, the people sat up. Heads lifted, and once-teary eyes brightened. *Jesus alive? How could this be?*

"The power of God inside Jesus raised Him back to life," the missionary told the wondering crowd.

Holding up the white, fluffy lamb that everyone understood as the substitute for sinners in the Old Testament, the missionary explained, "Abraham, he found a ram to sacrifice—not his son. God, He provided. God, He gave His Son, Jesus. He be our Lamb. He die instead of us. God, He accept Jesus' death. He save us." The missionary paused as he watched the truth sink in. "Do you believe?" he asked.

"It is true! It is true!" The words repeated through the crowd began like a ripple on the ocean waves but increased in volume. "It is true! It is true!"

Jumping from his bench, one of the leaders lifted his voice to the villagers, "I know I am a sinner. I know Jesus died in my place. He is my Sin Bearer!" His aging mother came to his side with waving arms, circling him in joy and patting him lovingly.

Another woman came forward. "I lived in fear trying to please the spirits, for I knew of no other way to be free from sin. Christ's blood and death is the payment for my sin." She raised her arms to heaven. "God has forgiven me. It is true!"

Nearly the whole village came forward to share their belief in Jesus as their Savior.

"If you believe," the missionary assured them, "your sins are forgiven."

As if a shaken can of soda had just exploded, the normally restrained people broke loose! Husbands embraced wives, brothers whirled each other around, girls lifted their faces and arms to the sky, laughing. Accompanied by rhythmic whoops and hollers, jubilant men took hold of the missionary, lifting him and rolling him back and forth on their shoulders. So profound was their sense of freedom from sin that their celebration continued for two and a half hours. Jesus had brought them liberty!

When the villagers learned about Jesus, God's Son, everything changed. How has knowing Jesus changed your life?

Digging in the Word

1. Isaiah 53 offers a detailed description of who the Messiah would be and what He would experience. After reading it, write three characteristics of the Messiah for which you're most grateful.
2. Why did God send His Son, Jesus, to the world, and what kind of life did He live? John 3:16, 17; 1 Peter 2:21, 22
3. To what New Testament person did the sacrificial lamb point, and what is the result of that sacrifice? John 1:29; 1 John 2:2, NLT
4. What was the result of Jesus' death and resurrection? Philippians 2:8–10

Not Ready for Heaven

By Rachel Whitaker Cabose

🌱 Faith Seed 10: The Experience of Salvation

When we accept God's gift of salvation, the Holy Spirit works in our lives to help us become more like Jesus.

"According to the prophecies of Daniel, Jesus will return in the year 1843." The visiting preacher, William Miller, spoke confidently. Twelve-year-old Ellen Harmon,* sitting in the audience with her friends, felt icy fear clutch her. If Mr. Miller was right, Jesus' coming was only three years away!

I'm not good enough to go to heaven, Ellen thought despairingly. *When Jesus comes back, I'll be lost!*

She didn't say much after the meeting. She didn't want her friends to know how hopeless she felt.

As Mr. Miller's meetings continued, Ellen became more and more convinced that Jesus was coming soon—and she wasn't ready. She wished someone could tell her exactly what she needed to do to be saved. But she was too embarrassed to ask.

The next summer, Ellen went with her parents to the Methodist camp meeting. *Maybe there I can find the answers I need*, she hoped.

Ellen was puzzled by some of the things she saw at the camp meeting. She peered into one tent where people were praying. Suddenly one man jumped to his feet. "Hallelujah!" he shouted at the top of his voice. "God has delivered me from sin!"

Others jumped up around him, shouting and clapping their hands. Suddenly a young woman slumped to the floor. "Do you think she's all right?" Ellen asked a woman standing nearby.

---

* Ellen is better known by her married name, Ellen White.

47

"Oh, it's wonderful!" the woman exclaimed. "The power of the Lord is resting on her. She has been sanctified by the Spirit!"

Ellen felt more confused than ever. *Is this what's supposed to happen when I accept Jesus into my life?* she wondered.

But then she heard a sermon that seemed to be aimed right at her. "Some of you think you need to make yourself worthy of God's favor before you claim His promise of salvation," the preacher said. "That's a fatal mistake! Don't depend on yourself. Just come to Him in faith."

Encouraged, Ellen went to the front with others who were seeking God. *Help, Jesus! Save me!* she pleaded silently.

Suddenly a wonderful feeling of happiness came over her. Jesus seemed so close, and she knew that He understood all her troubles and cared about her. A huge smile spread across her face.

Just then, one of the older women came toward her. "Dear child, have you found Jesus?" she asked. Ellen was about to say yes, but she didn't have a chance. "Indeed, you have!" the woman exclaimed. "His peace is with you. I see it in your face!"

As Ellen traveled home from the camp meeting, the grass seemed to be greener and the sky, a deeper blue. Even the birds seemed to be praising their Creator. Ellen said little, savoring the joy that warmed her heart.

Having committed her life to Christ, Ellen was eager to be baptized, as Jesus was. Some of the women from her Methodist church tried to convince her that going completely under the water wasn't necessary—a sprinkling would do just fine. But her pastor agreed to baptize Ellen and several others in Casco Bay, which washed the shores of their hometown of Portland, Maine.

The day of Ellen's baptism was windy, and waves crashed against the rocks as she picked her way across them. Despite the rough seas, Ellen felt at peace as she rose from the water. She was starting a new life!

But it wasn't long before Ellen started to worry about her salvation again. William Miller came back to Portland to preach about Jesus' coming—now, he believed, only a year away!

I'm still not ready to meet Jesus, Ellen thought. *I haven't become a perfect Christian yet. God won't save me unless I'm holy and sinless.*

Ellen's fears grew until she could hardly sleep. When her twin sister dozed off, Ellen would creep out of bed and kneel on the floor, silently begging God to forgive her.

Ellen believed that if she were lost, she would be tormented forever in hell. The horrible descriptions she had heard of the lake of fire terrified her. Sweat stood out on her forehead as she pictured herself sinking in endless waves of flame.

"Jesus, have mercy on me!" she begged in a hoarse whisper, not daring to wake her sister.

During this time, Ellen had a memorable dream. In her dream, she was sitting sadly with her face in her hands, wishing she could talk to Jesus personally. Suddenly a man stood before her. "Do you wish to see Jesus?" he asked. "He is here, and you can see Him if you desire it. Take everything you possess, and follow me."

Ellen eagerly gathered all her belongings and followed her guide up a steep, fragile stairway. At the top was a door, where the man told her to leave everything she had brought.

Stepping through the door, Ellen found herself face-to-face with Jesus! His kingly yet loving eyes seemed to see right into her deepest thoughts and feelings.

Ellen felt the urge to hide from His searching gaze, but then Jesus smiled and put His hand on her head. "Fear not!" He said.

Jesus' kind voice filled Ellen's heart with happiness she had never known before. Just being in Jesus' presence was heavenly!

All too soon, the guide opened the door, and it was time to leave. But before she went back down the stairway, the guide gave her a green cord, coiled up in a circle. "Keep this next to your heart," he said. "When you wish to see Jesus, take it out and stretch it to its full length. Don't let it stay coiled up for too long, or it may become tangled and hard to straighten."

Ellen awoke with new hope in her heart. She concluded that the green cord represented faith. *Maybe faith in God is what I need*, she thought.

Finally, Ellen decided to tell her mother about her fears. Her mother encouraged her to talk with Pastor Stockman, a preacher they both knew and trusted.

As Ellen told Pastor Stockman of her struggles, tears came to his eyes. "Ellen, I know there is hope for you," he said. "The very fact that you are worried about your sins means that the Holy Spirit is working on your heart, and you are listening!"

Ellen dared to smile a tiny bit.

Pastor Stockman reminded Ellen that Jesus had left heaven and given His own life so she could live forever. "God loves His children, even when they sin," he continued. "He doesn't want to destroy them—He wants to save them!"

The young preacher gently placed his hand on Ellen's head. "Go free, Ellen. Return to your home, trusting in Jesus. He will not withhold His love from any true seeker."

What We Believe

As Pastor Stockman prayed earnestly for Ellen, the fear that had gripped her heart melted like snow in the spring sunshine. She felt she had learned more about God's love in a few minutes than she had in her entire life! Never again would she see God as a cruel, scary dictator. At last, she could trust fully in His love and care for her.

Ellen was so excited about her newfound love for God that she couldn't help telling others about it. Even though she was extremely shy, she shared her testimony the very next day at a prayer meeting. She began praying for her friends and urging them to commit their lives to Jesus—and many did!

It was only a few years later that God called Ellen to serve as His special messenger. It was a difficult job, but through all the challenges she faced, she continued to rely on her loving heavenly Father.

Near the end of her life, Ellen wrote that all Christians experience discouraging times in their relationship with God. When that happens, she advised, "cling to Jesus. . . . Christ will never abandon those for whom He has died."[1]

Like Ellen, we can experience the joy of accepting God's grace and salvation. When we do, the Holy Spirit will help us grow our faith.

Digging in the Word

1. "Only Jesus has the power to save! His name is the only one in all the world that can save anyone" (Acts 4:12, CEV). To find out what sinners need to do once the Holy Spirit shows them their need for Christ's forgiveness (John 16:8), unscramble the underlined words. For clues, read Psalm 51:1–11. (Hint: What is David doing in this psalm?) nfcsoes and npteer
2. What does God do with His followers' sins? Jeremiah 31:34; Psalm 103:12; 1 John 1:9
3. Read Isaiah 1:18, and draw a picture of what you think forgiveness looks like.
4. What do you think being born again means? John 3:1–9
5. What does God do for us in order to save us? Ezekiel 36:26, 27; Colossians 1:13, 14, NLT
6. What can we do to know right from wrong? Psalm 119:11
7. In John 15:1–17, NLT, Jesus talks about remaining in Him. What do you think this means?

---

1. Ellen G. White, *Prophets and Kings* (Mountain View, CA: Pacific Press®, 1943), 175, 176.

Heal Him or Die

By Ellen Weaver Bailey

✐ Faith Seed 11: Growing in Christ

Salvation helps us see the world as Jesus sees it
and prompts us to make a difference for Him.

H ere he comes!"

"Welcome home, Jacobus!"

"Tell us all about the big city!"

Teenager Jacobus Bindosano had been away from his home village of Nubai for several months, working in the capital city of what is now West Papua, on the western end of the island of New Guinea. Now his wife, Johanna, and all his friends and relatives surrounded him to welcome him home. They clamored for news of the city, and they *oohed* and *aahed* over his reports of motorcars, big buildings, and busy docks.

"But I found something even better in the city," he informed those gathered around. "I learned about a man called Jesus, who died to save each one of us."

Everyone was eager to hear about this Jesus. Jacobus told them everything he could, patiently answering their many questions to the best of his ability.

"I don't know the answers to all your questions, but I know how to get them," he finally said. "*Pendita* [Pastor] Tilstra and Pendita Vijsma are offering a training course for Papuan youth so that we can become teachers and tell everyone in our villages about Jesus." This excited several of his friends, and five of them decided to go back with him to take the training course.

The steamship tickets would be expensive, and even though they were teenagers, most of them already had wives to provide for. It took time and lots of planning, saving, and determination, but eventually, all five young men raised the money. They said goodbye to their families and friends and set off on the slow, tedious journey.

The book *A Dutchman Bound for Paradise*, by Albertine Klingbeil Tilstra (Hagerstown, MD: Review and Herald®, 1980), was used as the resource for this story.

Heal Him or Die

One morning as Pendita Tilstra and his helpers were working on the church they were building, they were surprised to see six barefoot Papuan youths trudging up from the harbor in the hot sun. They were loaded down with clothing, sleeping nets, and woven palm bags containing a supply of the starchy sago that is still a staple food on New Guinea.

"Jacobus!" Pendita Tilstra exclaimed as he recognized the young man. "Welcome back! And who are your friends?" Jacobus introduced his companions and explained that they all wanted to learn more about the true God.

"But where is the school?" asked Jacobus's friend Abel Serami, looking around.

"We don't have a school yet," explained the missionary-pastor. "We are still building the church and a home for my wife and me. Then we will build a school with a dormitory for students."

"But we have come to attend school," Abel insisted, the other young men nodding in agreement. "You're a teacher, aren't you?" asked Abel. "Can't you use the church as a school and teach us right here?"

When he saw their determination, Pendita Tilstra did not have the heart to turn them away. *Yes,* he thought, *they can be taught in the back room of the unfinished church, but where will they live?* He and his wife were making do with a single room, ten feet by ten feet. They could not possibly cram all six teens into that tiny space along with them. There was only one answer.

"You will have to live in half of this back room," the pastor said, showing them the space. "We will hold school in the other half. Is that acceptable to you?"

Indeed it was! The teens quickly built a palm-leaf shelter outside the living area for a kitchen, while the missionaries divided up teaching duties.

The next day the students and Penditas Tilstra and Vijsma built desks. Soon the youths were deep into intensive study, using Malay-language Bibles as textbooks. Both pastors and their wives taught various subjects.

Several months later, after a formal graduation ceremony, the young men were eager to begin work.

Abel, with John Waramori, headed up into the mountains to work with the Arfak Papuans. Carrying packs loaded with supplies, books, and medicines, the two youths waded across crocodile-infested rivers, thanking their guardian angels for protecting them from the fierce reptiles.

After several days of walking, the two youths arrived in the village of Aimasse.

Many tribes lived in West Papua and Papua New Guinea, and each one had its own language. The new workers did not know the language of the Arfak Papuans, so they had to communicate with a mixture of Malay and sign languages. Regardless of the language problem, the people of Aimasse were happy to have these two "gurus" live among them. Soon a school for the children was organized.

The teachers had only one prerequisite. "You cannot come to school dirty," the two young teachers insisted. "All students must bathe first." The villagers objected.

"But Guru, the water is too cold for bathing before sunup!" they pointed out. Abel and John explained the importance of cleanliness for health and led by their own example. Each morning and evening, they bathed in the cold mountain stream. The villagers noticed the difference between their own skin disorders and the clear, healthy skin of the gurus, and slowly they learned to keep themselves clean.

The children eagerly worked at learning to read and write, and many adults slipped up quietly to listen to the lessons. Classes started early, followed by Bible study for everyone, aided by a picture roll. Then it was off to the gardens, where the young "gurus" demonstrated how to plant a variety of vegetables to improve health.

After lunch, the young teachers operated a mini dispensary, dressing wounds and handing out medicines. The dispensary became so popular that soon people were coming from all the surrounding villages.

One day, through the heavy morning mists, the youths noticed a line of armed strangers heading down the mountain toward Aimasse. At sunup, they reached the village.

"Where is the men's house?" they asked. "We want to see the two gurus from the coast." They were directed to the gurus' dwelling place. Displaying their spears and *parangs* (heavy knives similar to machetes), they directed a command at the young men. "Come with us! We have heard that you heal the sick in this *kampong* [village]. We have a sick man in our kampong. Come with us and heal him. You must not fail. If he dies, we will kill you!"

Abel and John asked for a few minutes to prepare, then went into the hut to consult.

"I'll go," said Abel. "You need to stay here so that if I don't come back, there will still be someone to help the Aimasse villagers." John, at last, agreed. Kneeling, the two young men prayed for forgiveness for their sins and asked for wisdom to care for the sick man. Then Abel packed a few quinine pills, vitamins, disinfectant, and bandages, hoping he was choosing the right items for the man's illness.

The moment Abel stepped outside the hut, the armed men hurried him away.

Heal Him or Die

It was a long and difficult trek, up and down mountain paths and through several rivers. The patient was obviously someone who was loved and respected.

When they finally arrived in the village of Maripi, Abel was led to a hut in which he found an old man, covered with dirt and pig grease, lying on a filthy mat and shaking with malarial chills. Between his shoulders festered an ulcer as big as a bread plate. Abel sent up a silent prayer and then turned to the villagers.

"You have brought me to heal this man," he said, "but I am just a man like you and can do nothing. The great God I serve is the one who will heal him. This great God likes things clean, so before I touch this man, you must clean up the hut and fetch some water so I can wash him." One woman grabbed a broom and began to sweep the hut and straighten up, while another hurried to get the water. Abel directed that some of the water be boiled.

After washing the patient, Abel took some of the boiled water and gently cleansed the ulcer. Then he applied a wet dressing and bandaged it securely, wrapping the bandage around the man's torso. He also administered a couple of quinine pills to calm the chills and fever and a vitamin pill to help strengthen the man's system. Then Abel rose to his feet and addressed the villagers.

"Now I will tell you about the great God," he announced. Using a picture roll, he told the villagers how Jesus healed the sick when He was on earth. He told them about the God who loved them and wanted to take them to His own home in heaven.

"God wants you to be clean. He wants you to love other people, not fight them. Now I will pray for the sick man. Get down on your knees with me, hold your hands like this, and close your eyes."

Wondering at this strange charm, the villagers did as they were told. They were very quiet as they rose from their knees after the prayer. Abel gave one of the man's relatives instructions on how to keep the patient clean and how to care for his wound.

"I am leaving now," said Abel. "I will return in two weeks." The villagers just stared at him in astonishment, and no one made a move to stop him as he left.

Two weeks later, Abel returned to the village. He was met by excited children chattering in their language. Unable to understand them, Abel just smiled and hurried to the old man's hut. To his surprise, his patient was standing outside the hut and came forward with a smile on his face and a hand outstretched in greeting.

Seeing no bandage, Abel turned the man around. There was no need for a bandage. Of the huge ulcer, only a quarter-sized spot remained. Eager villagers crowded around the young teacher.

"You have healed one of our fathers. We want to know more about the great God who loves and heals. Stay with us and tell us about Him."

Sadly, Abel shook his head. "I'm sorry," he said. "My work is in Aimasse. I must teach the children there." As the villagers' faces fell, he quickly added a promise. "I will ask the pendita to send a teacher to you."

As a result of the healing of this one man, a teacher did come to the village, where the people were eager to learn of the great Spirit in heaven. The Maripi villagers, who had once threatened to kill the teacher if he did not succeed, now had the opportunity to learn about eternal life.

Jacobus learned about Jesus and became His follower. When we do that, as we follow Jesus' example, we become more and more like Him in every area of life and we lovingly serve others and witness to Jesus' salvation.

Digging in the Word

1. Matthew 25:31-46 describes Christlike people and what they do for others while they wait for Jesus' return. How are you doing in these areas?
2. What do you think the psalmist meant in Psalm 77:11, 12 when he said that he'd remember the works of the Lord?
3. God's people are to be humble (Philippians 2:5-7), serving (Matthew 20:25-28), loving (John 13:35), and the kind of people who don't drink, are grateful, and sing to the Lord (Ephesians 5:18-20). What other quality characterizes Jesus' followers? Luke 10:17-20

The Giving Garden

By Jill Nogales

🌱 Faith Seed 12: The Church

Called to share the gospel, the church is God's family on earth,
serving, celebrating, studying, and worshiping together.

Hey, Ian!" Tanner called from the driveway. "Are you ready to go?"

Ian shoved a pair of gardening clippers into his backpack. Then he shut the garage door and hopped onto his bike. "Yep, let's go!"

"I wonder if the carrots are ready to be picked yet," Tanner said as they rode their bikes toward the church.

"Maybe," said Ian. "We can pull a few when we get there and find out."

Behind the church, there had been a large patch of dirt. Last spring Tanner and Ian had asked the pastor if they could make it into a vegetable garden. All summer, with the help of other kids in their youth group, they had been digging in the dirt, planting seeds, and pulling weeds. Now that the vegetables were becoming ripe, the kids had been picking them and sharing them with the people who lived in the neighborhood near the church. They called it the Giving Garden.

When they arrived at the church, Tanner and Ian leaned their bikes against a wooden shed and got to work. Ian clipped cucumbers and peppers while Tanner picked tomatoes and beans. Then they checked the carrots.

"Look at this." Tanner pulled up a fat orange carrot. "These are ready."

"Nice! Let's pick a bunch," Ian said.

When they were finished harvesting, they sorted the vegetables into cardboard boxes. Then they loaded the boxes onto the church's wagon and pulled it toward the homes in the neighborhood near the church. Tanner knocked on Mr. Sánchez's door first.

"Did you bring me some more of your church vegetables?" Mr. Sánchez asked hopefully.

Ian handed him a box. "We sure did. Here are fresh tomatoes for you and those hot peppers you like."

Mr. Sánchez smiled as he took the box. "This is just what I need to make a fine batch of salsa for my family. You've made my day!"

Ian knocked on old Mrs. Tuttle's door next. She slowly opened the door and peered out at them. "Hello, Mrs. Tuttle," Ian said. "Would you like some fresh vegetables from the church garden?"

The door opened wider, and Mrs. Tuttle looked in the box. "For me?" she asked.

Tanner nodded. "You like beans, cucumbers, and tomatoes, right?"

"I sure do. It's difficult for me to get to the grocery store these days, so I hardly ever get fresh vegetables anymore." Tears filled her eyes. "It sure is kind of you to bring these to me."

As Tanner and Ian approached the front door of the last house, they could hear fussing and crying. Tanner knocked, and a tired-looking mother with two young boys clinging to her legs opened the door.

"Mrs. Reed? We're sorry to bother you. We were just wondering if you would like some fresh vegetables from the church garden." Tanner held out the box so she could see inside. "There are cucumbers and beans and stuff."

Mrs. Reed nodded. "Sure. That would be nice. Come on in."

The little boys stopped crying and watched as Tanner put the box on the kitchen counter. "Do your boys like carrots?" Tanner asked. "I could help you wash a few, and then you can cook them for dinner. We just picked them today."

"That's a great idea," Mrs. Reed said. "Thank you."

While Tanner and Mrs. Reed worked in the kitchen, washing and trimming the vegetables, Ian sat on the couch with the boys. They listened quietly while he read a few books to them. Pretty soon, a pot of vegetables was simmering on the stove.

"You've been such a big help to me," Mrs. Reed said as she wiped her hands on a kitchen towel. "I'm so blessed to be living near your church."

"Come join us for worship sometime," Tanner said. "You are always welcome, you know."

"The church has a great nursery for the boys," Ian added.

Mrs. Reed nodded. "I think I'd like that."

A few days later, Tanner arrived early at church for Sabbath worship. As he was looking around for Ian, Tanner noticed that Mr. Sánchez was in church for the first time. The pastor was shaking Mr. Sánchez's hand and meeting his family.

The Giving Garden

Then Tanner saw Mrs. Tuttle! Two church ladies were welcoming her, and then they helped her find a seat in a nearby pew.

I wonder if Mrs. Reed will come to church today too, Tanner thought. He waited near the back and watched for her. But when the music started and there was no sign of her, he went to find his seat, feeling somewhat disappointed.

A few minutes later, the church door opened. Tanner looked back and saw Mrs. Reed and a man slip into the back pew. As soon as the service ended, Tanner hurried over to them. "I'm glad you came!" he said.

Mrs. Reed smiled. "Me too," she said. "I'd like you to meet my husband."

"You must be Tanner," Mr. Reed said. "My wife told me how kind you and your friend Ian have been to her. So I figured this church must be a good place."

"It was wonderful to be here today," Mrs. Reed said. "We would like to come again to worship God with you."

On the way home, Tanner couldn't stop smiling. God's loving presence was touching the lives of the neighborhood people, and it had all started with a patch of dirt.

Tanner and Ian were God's church to their community when they served their neighbors by sharing and delivering produce to them.

Digging in the Word

1. Fill in the blanks:
   "Christ is _____ of the _____; and He is the _____ of the _____"
   (Ephesians 5:23).
2. How does Peter describe God's church in 1 Peter 2:9?
3. In Hebrews 10:24, 25, *The Message*, the author encourages the church do the following:
   "Let's keep a firm grip on the _____ that keep us going. [God] always keeps his _____. Let's see how inventive we can be in _____ _____ and _____ _____, not avoiding _____ _____ as some do but spurring each other on, especially as we see the big Day approaching."

The Girl Who Lost Her Family

By Elfriede Volk

🌱 Faith Seed 13: The Remnant and Its Mission

While God's people are waiting for Jesus' soon return,
God asks them to share the special truths found in Revelation 14:6–12.

As twelve-year-old Lily and Father walked home after the opera, the strains of the opera kept playing in her mind.

"I now know what I want to be," she said.

"A good girl?"

"No, I . . ."

"What? You don't want to be good?" Father asked in mock surprise.

"Oh, Daddy! Of course I want to be good, but I also want to be an opera singer."

"You'd have to move abroad to study," Father said thoughtfully.

Lily wondered with excitement what it would be like to go somewhere outside of Poland for school. Her family was originally from Germany. Would Father send her to school there?

Nothing more was said that evening, but Lily noticed that Father seemed to be preoccupied. Was it the political unrest?

"Don't believe everything you hear," he said at breakfast one morning. "There are many false rumors going around."

"Like that we're heading for another war?" Mother asked.

"That's one of them," Father said. "And be careful whom you trust, and what you say. Some people pretend to be friends—but then betray you."

"Like Judas did to Jesus?" asked Markus, Lily's younger brother.

"Exactly," Father said, ruffling his son's hair. "Judas wanted Jesus to get rid of the Romans. In our case, because Germans and Poles have not always been friends, there are still some Poles who want all Germans out of the country."

The Girl Who Lost Her Family

By midsummer, Father had indeed found a school in Germany to send Lily to. With promises to visit often, Father ordered a taxi so the whole family could go to the train station to see her off.

Welcome to the school of culture and music," Herr Meyer said as the bell signaled the beginning of classes. "So I can get to know each of you personally, I want you to write an essay on your goals in life."

Lily frowned. She remembered Father's words: "Be careful what you say." Herr Meyer was a total stranger. Would it be safe to disclose her heart's desire? Or did he have an ulterior motive?

Herr Meyer looked at Lily. "Do you understand, *fräulein*, or do I need to repeat the instructions in Polish?"

The entire class snickered.

"No, I understand," she said, turning red. She picked up her pen and began writing.

"My goals are quite simple," she wrote. "I don't like hard work, so I will just marry a farmer and have a half dozen kids." Then she handed her paper in.

That was Wednesday, August 30. It was also her birthday, the day she officially became a teenager. After the hype of being in a new country and new school, she felt terribly let down. She never realized that she would miss her parents and brother so much.

Friday, September 1, was even worse. That was when Germany broke its agreement and invaded Poland. Sixteen days later, Russia attacked from the other side. Then it became a free-for-all, with many nations in the world joining in.

Lily was not concerned about world politics. She was only worried about her family, caught between two invading armies. She wanted to know that they were safe. She had written her parents but received no answer. Travel was impossible, and the mail and phone service were disrupted. There was no way she could contact them or that they could contact her. France, Great Britain, and Russia joined the war against Germany, and with new weapons and air raids, there was no place that was safe.

Lily lost track of time as days became nightmares. The war against Poland ended, but the war against Germany intensified as the United States also joined in. Schools closed, including the one Lily attended. In fact, the entire town was evacuated. Somehow Lily made it to the train station, dragging her suitcase.

"Get on board, fräulein," a male voice commanded.

"I can't," Lily said. "There's no room."

The train was crammed full. People were even standing on the steps outside the open doors, desperately hanging on to anything they could to keep from falling off. A soldier marched to Lily's side and pounded on the train window. "Open up!" he shouted.

A man inside struggled with the latch, then raised the window. What happened next was so fast that it took Lily's breath away. The soldier picked her up and shoved her headfirst through the opening. Before she even got her feet on the floor, her suitcase came in the same way, just as the train chugged out of the station.

Lily ended up in Berlin, where she searched for rags in the rubble of basements and bunkers. When washed, they could be sold. Reaching for a pair of pants, she was shocked to find a dead body inside. Her scream brought another girl running.

"We'll have to report this to the authorities," the girl said.

But the British sergeant they found could not understand them. "Do you speak English?" he asked.

"A little," Lily replied.

"Good. You can be my interpreter."

As an interpreter, Lily was able to make contact with the Red Cross and other agencies that tried to reunite families. She found her beloved Aunt Jenny and Maria, but there was no word about her parents or brother.

The girl who had helped Lily report her grisly find stayed in touch with her and invited her to church and to join the choir. The pastor there was approachable, not like the standoffish clergymen she had met before.

"Why can't I find my parents?" she asked him. "Even if they are dead, I want to know."

"I can understand your pain," the pastor said, "and God can too. Jesus also wept at His friend's tomb."

"I'll never forget them, never quit searching for them,"* Lily said, as if to herself.

"Nor should you. You are a survivor. God kept you alive for a purpose. Our heavenly Father also has many children who became separated from Him. That's why Jesus came to this world. His mission was 'to seek and to save that which was lost' [Luke 19:10]. And when He returned to His Father, He entrusted that mission to us."

Little by little, the pastor introduced Lily to her heavenly Father. At her baptism,

---

* Lily's diligent search efforts yielded some results. Though she did not find her parents, she did find several members of her extended family.

she was adopted by the entire church family.

The war may have separated her from her earthly father, but there was no power on earth that would be able to separate her from her heavenly Father and the new family He had given her.

When she was separated from her family, Lily became one of the few people to escape her country. She embarked on a lifelong mission to find relatives around the world. God's remnant church's few members escape this sinful planet. While on the earth, their mission includes a lifelong dedication to telling people around the world about Jesus' love so they, too, can become a part of His church.

Digging in the Word

1. How does Revelation 14:12 describe the remnant (saints)?
2. Unscramble the underlined words to find out what Jesus asks the remnant to do before He comes: Be a idwerlwod setwins. (Matthew 28:19, 20)
3. What is the invitation for the remnant? Revelation 18:2-4

The Casket in Church

By Bernardo Sámano

🍃 Faith Seed 14: Unity in the Body of Christ

Church members are called to work together
to advance God's work on the earth.

By the time the hearse arrived, boys and girls, adults and the elderly, had occupied every pew in the church until there was no room left to be seated. Even the balcony of the Mexican church was packed, and people stood in the hallways. There were lots of black suits and white dresses, and many people were wearing sunglasses; maybe they had been sobbing and were covering up their swollen eyes. But, believe it or not, except for a handful of people in the crowded church, nobody knew who had died.

At the end of his sermon that morning, Pastor Ruiz* had simply announced there was going to be a funeral service later in the afternoon, and he had encouraged everybody to attend. After making announcements and offering the closing prayer, Pastor Ruiz had mysteriously disappeared.

"Who died?" everyone asked.

"Maybe Brother Juan or what's her name . . . Sister Mary?" A lot of hypotheses arose.

"Maybe Mrs. Rodríguez. She has been struggling with cancer for so long," said someone.

"No," somebody else chimed in. "I am sure that Mr. López died. He's not been attending church for many months."

"Let's ask Pastor Ruiz," somebody else suggested.

However, the pastor was nowhere to be found.

---

* Names have been changed.

The Casket in Church

That afternoon, lots of sick members, shut-ins, nonattending members, and back-sliders received surprise visits from church members who were trying to figure out who had died.

What a day it was! Many church members' confused faces now wore smiles as they were happy to see people they hadn't seen in a long time.

Visits to those who were sick had to be cut short because everybody wanted to attend the mysterious funeral. Soon dozens of people headed toward the church, curious to find out who had died.

The building was so full that it was as if the church were holding Sabbath morning camp meeting. Nobody wanted to miss the opportunity of supporting a friend in a time of loss. All the choir members wore their black gowns, and the choir director had them ready and warmed up before three o'clock. This time, even the talkative teenagers were quiet.

The deacons made sure all the lights and fans were in working condition. For the first time in many months, all of them were wearing their uniforms and badges indicating their office. With solemn gestures, the deacons ushered everybody, silently making sure every space was filled.

Filled with floral arrangements, the platform looked as if the Garden of Eden had been transplanted to the church. The fancy ribbons on the flowers indicated a variety of condolence messages from neighboring churches. On the floor, right below the pulpit, a bright bronze casket carriage awaited the arrival of the dead body. Around it, like soldiers on guard, four tall lamps stood, lighting everything around them. The deacons organized themselves as pallbearers, for they knew not who was going to take the casket out of the hearse and into the church.

The pianist's crescendos and diminuendos had never been played with such spiritual depth in the history of piano playing. The piano's black and white keys' melodies led every member to reflect on how fragile human lives are.

"Mmm mmm mmm mmm," attendees hummed the melodies.

Finally, right on time, the hearse arrived. The deacons did a wonderful job! Eight deacons lowered the casket and walked with military precision into the church. As soon as the casket appeared in the lobby, the music director started to lead such songs as "Amazing Grace," "The Old Rugged Cross," and "Abide With Me." Many tears rolled out of the eyes of those who were present. It was an unprecedented moving experience.

"Mommy, why are you crying?" a ten-year-old asked, tears welling up in her own eyes.

"Someone died, honey."

"Who?"

"I don't know." Mother hugged her daughter and dried her tears.

The very few who knew the details regarding the funeral service were scattered among the congregation, quiet, waiting. When the music stopped, Pastor Ruiz and some of the elders walked up to the platform.

"On behalf of the family of our brother who now rests in the Lord, we want to thank you very much for your presence and support," said one of the elders.

The congregation sang another hymn, an elder offered the opening prayer, and Pastor Ruiz stood and invited the congregation to stand and line up to offer their respects and see the dead church member for the last time.

The ones who knew who it was encouraged those around them to stand and go. Pastor Ruiz stood at the front of the line and opened the upper part of the casket so those coming up to the casket would be able to see the face of the deceased. One after another, everyone walked with heavy hearts, some dragging their feet. But most of them, curious, lined up single file and started to march toward the open casket.

When the church members peeked inside, some gasped, others shed tears, and younger ones, including thirteen-year-old Carlos and ten-year-old Juanita, covered their mouths to prevent giggles from escaping or to mask their smiles. Others were surprised and upset as they saw their own face reflected in a mirror. There was a sign below the mirror that said, "You are the dead one."

When the viewing ended, Pastor Ruiz got up to speak. "Please be seated."

There was a lot of talking.

"May I have your attention, please?" Pastor Ruiz requested gently. Finally, when everybody was quiet, Pastor Ruiz continued. "Open your Bibles to Revelation three, verse one." He paused to give the congregation time to find the verse. "I know your works, that you have a name that you are alive, but you are dead."

During the months prior to the funeral, the church had been split in half. There had been a lack of unity, especially among the teenagers and the youth. All the youth programs were well organized, but when group A had prepared a program, the members of group B had not attended. And when group B had been in charge, group A had not attended. Young adults and adults were also guilty of this.

"We cannot get to heaven this way," Pastor Ruiz said. "How can we fulfill Jesus' prayer when He said, 'That they also may be one in Us, that the world may believe that You sent Me' [John 17:21]? We will not make it, not this way. We must work shoulder to shoulder, with the power of the Holy Spirit, and share the good news with family members, our neighbors, classmates, fellow workers, friends, and the world.

"We need to set our differences aside, forgive each other, affirm each other, support each other, and follow Jesus' marching orders to 'go therefore and make disciples' [Matthew 28:19]. If we aren't united, if we don't accept what the Spirit says to the churches, we all will perish. 'Hold fast and repent' [Revelation 3:3]," Pastor Ruiz concluded.

That was a turnaround moment. The church accepted the invitation. The congregation cried, but this time they were tears of joy. They hugged, and lots of people prayed with and for one another.

Soon the youth of the local church became leaders and organized a statewide youth federation, and the elders organized the church into evangelistic groups. As a result, the church was soon divided, but this time it was not because of differences among them but because they had grown so much that they had to start another church a couple of miles away.

———————————

Just like Pastor Ruiz's church could not function when it was divided, so it is with the worldwide church. Though there is diversity, we are equal in Jesus, and we are to fellowship with Jesus and with one another, serve one another, and witness to everyone.

Digging in the Word

1. Read Psalm 133 in two or three Bible versions. To what would you compare "dwelling together in unity"?
2. When the church is united, whose example is it following? John 17:20-23
3. Read Romans 12:4, 5 and 1 Corinthians 12:12-14. Why, do you think, it is important to have different kinds of people in the church?
4. What motivates Christians' unity? Matthew 28:19; Acts 1:11; Ephesians 2:13-16; Galatians 3:26-29

Baptized in a Bucket

By Lawrence Maxwell

🕊 Faith Seed 15: Baptism
Baptism shows others that you trust in
Jesus' forgiveness and have chosen to follow Him.

Buckets were used for the baptism because there wasn't anything else available, and the Kalbermatter family were determined to be baptized.

The missionary spoke to the family sitting in front of him. "We have finished our series of Bible studies," he said. "Are you willing to follow Jesus?"

"I am," Mother said.

"So are we," several of the others said.

"I'm so happy," the minister said solemnly. "Is there a river or lake nearby with enough water in which to conduct the baptismal service?"

"Down the well is the only place I know of," piped up Little Brother.

Mother was shocked. She looked sternly at Little Brother. It was embarrassing to have him say such a silly thing.

The missionary just smiled. "No, no, little one," he said. "That would never do. We need a river or a lake. Mrs. Kalbermatter," he said to Mother, "is there not a lake or river nearby?"

Slowly Mother shook her head.

"You see," big sister explained, "here on the Argentine pampas where we live, you can go for miles and miles and miles and never find even a stream."

"What shall we do?" asked the missionary.

"Perhaps we'll have to follow Little Brother's suggestion," Big Brother said.

They went out and looked at the well, Little Brother trailing behind.

"Pretty dark down there," Sister observed.

"And how would we reach the water?" the missionary asked.

"Oh, there's plenty of rope," Big Brother said, "and there are two buckets."

"How about it, Sister Kalbermatter?" the missionary asked. "Would you be afraid?"

"No." She smiled. "It's all right, just so long as I can follow Jesus."

"Then we'll have the baptism in the well," the missionary decided. And Little Brother grinned all over.

I suppose they sang a hymn and the minister led in prayer. Then he stepped into one of the buckets, and Big Brother let out the rope, lowering him farther and farther until the water was up to his waist.

"Far enough," the minister called. Then one of the members of the family stepped into the other bucket. Big Brother let him down till he was waist deep in water too, and then the minister baptized him. He was pulled to the top, and another member of the family went down. And so it went till all were baptized.

That really took place many years ago in Argentina. The Kalbermatters were determined to follow Jesus and would not let anything stand in their way.

How about you? Are you letting something stand in the way of your being baptized? If you're old enough, don't put it off.

The Kalbermatter family chose to get baptized to show that they had faith in Jesus. They were baptized and fully immersed in the well water as a symbol of dying to their past life and resurrecting to a new life in Jesus, thus accepting salvation.

Digging in the Word

1. According to Matthew 3:13-17, whom did John baptize, and how did he do that? Why do you think this is meaningful for believers?
2. What needs to happen before a person gets baptized? Acts 2:38
3. What does baptism symbolize? Romans 6:1-4
4. Why is it important to be fully submerged in water when one is baptized? Colossians 2:12, 13

Belief Bonus: The primary meaning of the Greek word for baptism, *baptizo*, which Paul used in Ephesians 4:5, is "to dip repeatedly, to immerse, to submerge."[1]

---

1. New Testament Greek Lexicon, Bible Study Tools, s.v. "baptizo" https://www.bible studytools.com/lexicons/greek/nas/baptizo.html.

Clean Feet

By Monica Frede

🌱 Faith Seed 16: The Lord's Supper

The Lord's Supper symbolizes our acceptance of the body and blood
of Jesus. By searching our hearts and washing one another's feet, we
remember Jesus' humble example of service.

D o you hear something?" I whispered to my three friends in a shaky, scared voice.
On this muggy July night, my friends and I were walking arm in arm down a dirt
path. The pitch-black sky kept us from seeing anything, and we huddled together to
stay away from the edges of the path.

Chelsea whispered back to me, "No, I don't hear anything. What did you hear?"

I didn't know what I had heard. I decided maybe my mind was playing a trick on
me. But then—

Crunch, crunch, crunch. I heard the noise again. It was a faint sound of crunching
leaves, as if a large animal were walking slowly through the trees.

"There! Right there! Did you hear it?" I squeezed two different arms.

Stacey chimed in, "I heard it that time!"

The four of us froze in midstride. We wanted to turn around and run back to the
cabin where our youth pastor and the rest of our youth-group friends were playing
games. Instead, we pressed on.

"Let's keep going. I'm sure it's nothing." I didn't believe myself, and I know they
didn't believe me either, but we wanted to prove the boys wrong. The boys in our
youth group had tried to scare us when we had announced that we were going to
take the short walk to our tent—alone. They had warned us about wild bears and
slithering snakes.

"They'll bite your toes!"

"Yeah, and tackle you with their big paws!"

The boys had laughed and tried to convince us that walking to our tent would prove dangerous. But we needed to retrieve our Bibles for the night's activity in the cabin, and our pastor had told us to get them and hurry back.

Now, with the strange noise in the woods and the darkness surrounding us, we regretted our choice. We slid our feet cautiously along the ground, kicking up chunks of dry dirt with our flip-flops. We crept along the path until we saw the silhouette of our large tent. We sprinted to the front of it, and I unzipped the door. We toppled over each other to get inside so no one would be left standing outside by herself.

Rupp, shuup, crush.

"Now what was that?" Mary's voice began quivering. The noise got closer and closer to the tent.

"Let's just get our Bibles and get out of here!" I frantically searched for my Bible, running my hands over the backpacks, crumpled sleeping bags, and empty pretzel bags.

Then my hand felt something squishy. I felt it one second, but the next, it was gone. Before I could think about what I must have packed in my suitcase that felt slimy and cold, Mary squealed.

"A frog! There's a frog in my sleeping bag!" I could see an outline of her body and curly hair bouncing up and down.

"Ew! There's a frog in my suitcase!" Stacey pushed her suitcase away and let out a scream. Suddenly I knew what I had felt with my hand.

"Where are they coming from?" somebody screeched.

All four of us sprinted for the exit, pushing each other to get out just as quickly as we had pushed each other to get in moments before. We huddled together, whimpering and listening to the dozens of short, deep croaks harmonizing like a band of trombones.

Croooak, croooak, crooooak!

From inside a clump of bushes, we heard a faint giggling. The boys from our youth group crawled out, holding their stomachs as they howled with laughter at our petrified reactions.

"You did this? Why?" I pointed my finger toward their faces, but instead of responding, they ran down the dirt path toward the cabin, laughing all the way. With one glance at each other, we took off at a full sprint to chase after them.

During our run, we plotted our revenge.

"They'll be in so much trouble when we tell what they did!"

"I'm never talking to them again!"

"Let's fill their tent with snakes!"

Clean Feet

"Yeah! And then let's put mud in their shampoo bottles and dirt in their pancake batter!"

We reached the cabin and saw our youth pastor standing outside the front door.

"Pastor Steve! Pastor Steve!" Breathless, we simultaneously shouted his name. We could hear singing and laughing coming from inside the cabin as our friends played with instruments and board games.

But before we could tell him what had happened, he lifted his arm in the air and gave us the universal "stop" signal with the palm of his hand. He then tilted his head toward a shallow bucket filled with water that sat at his feet.

Puzzled, I ignored the water bucket. "But the boys just—"

He shook his head slowly from side to side and sat down in the folding chair that fit between the wall of the cabin and the water bucket.

He softly spoke. "Take off your sandals."

Confused, I turned to my friends. Chelsea popped her head over my shoulder. "But Pastor Steve, the boys put frogs in our tent, and—"

Instead of reacting to the news, Pastor Steve repeated himself. "Please take off your sandals."

This time we listened. We slid our flip-flops from our dirty feet. Pastor Steve leaned forward and picked up my right foot. He set it gently in the warm water and began washing my foot with the rag he held in his hands. He then motioned for me to put my other foot in the bucket.

Once my feet were clean, he handed me a towel. I stood silently. He looked up at me and softly said, "Regardless of what you have done, I wash your feet—just as Jesus washed the feet of His disciples."

He motioned for me to walk into the cabin. Then he washed the dirty feet of Chelsea, Mary, and Stacey.

I felt ashamed that Pastor Steve had washed my dirty feet. I didn't deserve that. My friends and I had wanted to play a prank on the boys and treat them the way they had treated us. We had wanted them to get into trouble and be punished for what they did. Pastor Steve knew how mad we felt, and he knew what the boys had done to us, but he had washed my feet anyway.

A few minutes later, the boys walked into the cabin with feet as clean as ours. Pastor Steve had washed their feet too!

As they walked toward us, I gave them each a smile. They smiled back at us. And on that hot July night, I learned that forgiveness is much more powerful than revenge.

Pastor Steve was willing to wash the girls' and boys' feet regardless of what they'd done. When Jesus established the foot-washing service and washed undeserving disciples' feet, it was to symbolize the sinner's renewed cleansing and desire to serve others in humility.

Digging in the Word

1. Christians follow the example of the Lord's Supper for the Communion service. Read Matthew 26:17–30 and 1 Corinthians 10:16, 17. In your journal, write about how you might have felt if you'd been one of the twelve disciples.
2. During the Last Supper, Jesus used _____ to symbolize His _____ and _____ _____ to symbolize His _____ (Matthew 26:26–28).
3. What does Jesus promise to those who eat the bread of life? John 6:47–51
4. What are Christians doing when they eat the bread and drink from the cup? 1 Corinthians 11:23–26
5. More than just a social activity, Communion should prompt Christians to take time to do what before participating? Matthew 5:23–24; 1 Corinthians 11:28

Logan's Choice

By Crystal Earnhardt

⌒ Faith Seed 17: Spiritual Gifts and Ministries

From art to teaching and listening to preaching, the Holy Spirit gives each
of us skills and talents to use for God's glory and the church's mission.

Logan sat in church, watching the pastor pace across the platform, occasionally
raising his arms or bending low to emphasize a point. "People are making decisions
every day," he said, "either for God or against Him." He paused for effect. "And
most of you are too complacent to care."

And how does he know whether we care or not? Logan thought as he shifted around on
the pew. *And what does "complacent" mean, anyway?* He never did like vocabulary class.
He glanced at his watch. Ten minutes! He should be done in ten minutes.

Mom frowned at him. Logan turned his attention straight ahead, pretending to
be interested.

"The church board has planned a series of meetings to share God with our
community," Pastor Ken said as he laid his Bible down on the pulpit. "We need
everyone's help, young and old."

Hmm, Logan thought, *I could work in the media room adjusting the microphones.* But
then he remembered the last time he tried to adjust the sound system during a
sermon. The blast was so high that it almost lifted the wig off old Mrs. Knox's head.
Pastor Ken stumbled backward on the pulpit, and a baby woke up screaming. Logan
was sure no one would let him within thirty feet of the media room again. In fact,
he was pretty sure there was a big sign on the soundboard: "Logan, do not touch!"

At last, the sermon ended, and people filed toward the door. He stopped to speak
to a few of his friends and then hurried to catch up with his family.

"Yes! I'm sure he would be glad to work in the children's class," he heard his
mother telling Mrs. Knox at the door.

Logan froze. Children's room! The worst but most necessary job in the whole church! There would be little kids running all over the place, screaming, throwing toys, and jabbering words that no one could understand. Mom was supposed to be looking out for him, not throwing him into a den of little monsters!

He whined about it all the way home from church, but Mom was adamant. "Everything is easier if everyone helps. You are a member of this church too!" Then Mom explained how the church is compared to a human body. Every part is important and works together, even small parts, including fingers and toes. "So if you are as little as a fingernail," she concluded, "then be the best fingernail you can be."

Logan thought of that comment all week. He attended every Sabbath, but he had never thought that working for the church was his responsibility, or "privilege," as Mom put it. *If I have to babysit*, he thought, *then I'll be the very best babysitter that I can be.*

Hmmm . . . what makes a good babysitter? He decided to go into the garage, where Mom had stored his old toys. He searched through them until he found his coolest ones—a wind-up rabbit, a remote-controlled fire truck, his little sister's jump rope that lit up when used, a large tub of Lincoln Logs, and some talking books.

When the meetings began, the adults met in the church auditorium, but the children's program took place in the fellowship hall. The children's leader opened the program with action songs, which most of the visitors' children didn't know. Logan remembered the actions, so he stood up with her even though he knew that most of his friends would laugh if they saw him marching in place or holding his finger up like a little light. Surprisingly, all the kids followed him instead of her.

Just then, the door opened, and a woman came in practically dragging a screaming little boy behind her. "I'm sorry," she apologized. "I really want to hear what the speaker is saying, but Devon won't sit still, so I can't hear anything."

"Of course," Mrs. Knox said as she hurried toward Devon, but the sight of a stranger coming at him caused Devon to scream louder. Mrs. Knox stopped, not knowing how she could help.

Suddenly Logan got an idea. He opened his box and pulled out his fire truck. He turned on the flashing lights and drove it toward the little boy, who quit crying immediately. "Come over here with me, and we will play with it after our story," Logan offered.

Devon's mother smiled. "He loves fire trucks. Thank you!"

Mrs. Knox was noticeably relieved. "Who would have guessed?" she clucked under her breath.

Logan's Choice

The nights slowly passed. Logan found himself hurrying home from school to get his schoolwork done so he could go to the meetings. He hated to admit it, but he almost enjoyed seeing how Devon's face lit up when he walked into the church. Other kids flocked around him too.

"You have really made a difference," Mom told him. "What would have happened if you hadn't been there that first night to keep Devon from crying? His mom would probably have gone home and not heard all the sermons from the Bible. Now the family is coming to church. Good job, Logan!"

Logan grinned. "Well, maybe next time I can work in the media room."

"Maybe one day," she laughed, "but first, we'll have to figure out how to get that sign off the wall that says, 'Logan, don't touch!'"

Logan unexpectedly found his gift for interacting with kids. He found that he enjoyed serving his church with it, and the Holy Spirit used him to minister to church members.

Digging in the Word

1. Read Acts 6:1-7 and 1 Corinthians 12:4-12. (a) What did the early church do in response to the need that they saw among fellow believers? (b) To what does Paul compare the church, and what do you think that means?
2. Who gives spiritual gifts? How and why are they distributed? 1 Corinthians 12:7-12, NLT
3. Which of the gifts listed in Romans 12:6-8 do you think God has given you? If you don't yet know, ask the Lord to show you. When He does, don't neglect using it (see 1 Timothy 4:14).

Silencing the Scoffers

By Rachel Whitaker Cabose

🥚 Faith Seed 18: The Gift of Prophecy

The Holy Spirit has blessed God's end-time people with the gift
of prophecy. One who demonstrated this gift was Ellen White,
a founder of the Seventh-day Adventist church.

It should have been a joyful worship service with fellow believers. But the atmosphere of the crowded parlor in Randolph, Massachusetts, was anything but friendly.

Ellen Harmon* and her sister Sarah could feel the curious stares and critical glares from other worshipers. They clearly were not welcome in this group.

The trouble had started a few months earlier, when seventeen-year-old Ellen had traveled to Randolph to talk about the visions God had given her. At first, the Adventist believers, still recovering from the Great Disappointment, had been thrilled by her message. But then the group's leaders had condemned Ellen's visions as satanic. "Her friend James White hypnotizes her," they had said. "She can't have a vision without him around."

It didn't help that Ellen had spoken out against the strange teachings of these leaders. They believed that Jesus had returned to earth "spiritually," starting a new millennium of rest, and it was now a sin to work!

But some people in Massachusetts believed that God was speaking through Ellen. One of them was Otis Nichols, who lived near Boston. Mr. Nichols had invited Ellen and Sarah to visit again, hoping Ellen could convince his friends that they were wrong.

A few days after Ellen had returned, Mr. Sargent and Mr. Robbins, two of the Adventist leaders who were most hostile to Ellen's visions, showed up at the Nichols home. "We came to visit your family and pray with you," they told Mr. Nichols.

---

* Ellen is better known by her married name, Ellen White.

"Wonderful!" Mr. Nichols replied with a grin. "Ellen Harmon and her sister Sarah are staying with us. You'll have a chance to get better acquainted!"

Mr. Sargent and Mr. Robbins looked at each other uncomfortably. "Well . . ." Mr. Sargent stammered, "we can't stay long. We must be back to Boston before dark."

"Don't be taken in by that girl," Mr. Robbins added in a low tone. "Her visions are of the devil."

" 'By their fruits ye shall know them' [Matthew 7:20, KJV]," Mr. Nichols shot back. "From all I can see, Sister Harmon is a young woman of excellent moral character. Her messages agree with the Bible and lead people to live holy lives."

"Humph!" snorted Mr. Robbins.

"Sister Harmon would like to attend your meeting in Boston next week," Mr. Nichols went on. "Would you have any opposition to hearing her testimony?"

"No, no, none at all," Mr. Sargent said hurriedly. "Let her come."

"And now we really must be on our way," his friend put in. The two men mounted their horses and rode off.

The night before the meeting in Boston, as Ellen and Sarah were praying with the Nichols family, Ellen received a vision with surprising news. "God has shown me that we should go to Randolph tomorrow instead of Boston," Ellen told the others. "He has a work for us to do there."

"But Mr. Sargent and Mr. Robbins need to hear your message!" Sarah protested.

"They'll hear it, all right," Ellen said with a frown. "In the vision, God showed me that they've decided to trick us. They told their whole group to meet in Randolph instead of Boston because they don't want their followers to listen to me."

"Oh!" Sarah exclaimed.

"God promised to give me a message tomorrow that will convince everyone with an honest heart whether my visions are from God or Satan," Ellen added.

The next morning they all headed to Randolph. When they arrived at the Thayer home, where the Adventist meetings were held, the service was already underway. Mr. Sargent and Mr. Robbins were up front, leading out.

When the two men saw Ellen and her group, they looked at each other in shock. "Oh, no!" groaned Mr. Sargent. The preacher was so flustered that he ended his sermon early.

During the break, Mr. Robbins cornered Sarah. "Your sister can't have a vision if I'm here!" he boasted.

The afternoon program began with songs and prayers. As Ellen prayed aloud, her voice suddenly changed to an odd, shrill tone. "Glory to God! Glory to God!" she said.

"She's having a vision!" Mr. Nichols exclaimed.

Instantly the congregation was abuzz. All eyes turned toward Ellen as she rose and began to walk around the room. "The teachers are teaching error. They are leading many astray," she said loudly and clearly. "But truth will triumph in the end."

"This is the work of the devil!" Mr. Robbins shouted, pointing a trembling finger toward the young woman, who seemed oblivious to everyone around her.

The worshipers shifted nervously in their seats. Mr. Sargent leaped to his feet. "Let's all sing 'Watch, Ye Saints,'" he announced, launching into the hymn without a pause. Some in the congregation joined in hesitantly, while others were too stunned to utter a note.

Mr. Sargent led one hymn after another, frantically trying to drown out Ellen's voice. Finally, he sat down, mopping his brow with a handkerchief. Mr. Robbins strode to the front and read a long Bible passage, commenting occasionally in his loudest preacher voice. Then the two sang more hymns.

"You're doing no good," one man finally interrupted. "The girl is still in vision. Why don't you stop and let us listen to what she is saying?"

Mr. Robbins's eyes bulged with anger. "You are bound to an idol!" he screeched. "You are worshiping a golden calf!"

Mr. Thayer, in whose home they were meeting, spoke up. "I'm not fully satisfied that these visions are of the devil, as you keep telling us. I think we should put it to the test. I've heard that if someone is having a satanic vision, laying an open Bible on them will stop the vision. Why don't you try that?"

"No, no—that's just a superstition," scoffed Mr. Sargent, a touch of worry in his voice.

"Well, I'm going to try it myself," Mr. Thayer announced. He picked up a large family Bible from a table and walked over to Ellen, who by this time was seated in a corner, leaning back against the wall. Mr. Thayer carefully laid the heavy Bible on her chest. "Now we'll see what happens," he said.

No one in the room dared to breathe. Even Mr. Sargent and Mr. Robbins fell silent.

The frail teenager effortlessly lifted the heavy Bible and stood to her feet. She walked to the center of the room and held the open Bible up on one hand, as high as she could reach. "The inspired testimony of God," she said.

Ellen turned some pages and pointed to a text. " 'I will send mine anger upon thee, and will judge thee according to thy ways' [Ezekiel 7:3, KJV]," she said.*

She flipped to the back of the Bible. " 'Behold, the judge standeth before the door' [James 5:9, KJV]," she proclaimed.

"Is she actually reading those verses?" a woman whispered.

"No, she's looking up at the ceiling, not at the Bible," a friend whispered back. "She couldn't see the words anyway—not with the Bible above her head."

"Somebody look to see if the text that she is pointing to is the one that she is saying," the first woman demanded.

Mr. Thayer obligingly stood on a chair so he could read along as Ellen spoke the next text. "Sure enough—she's pointing to that exact verse!" he marveled. "But how could she turn to the right spot without looking?"

Others in the crowd took turns standing on the chair as Ellen quoted verse after verse. Each one seemed to be an arrow of truth aimed directly at the wrong teachings of the group's leaders.

"What I want to know," the first woman whispered again, "is how she can hold up that Bible for so long. I should think her arm would be worn out by now."

No one answered. Some were listening in awed silence to Ellen. Others sat with eyes closed to block out the troubling scene.

By now, Ellen had been in vision for nearly four hours. With evening approaching, Mrs. Thayer lit candles around the room.

Unexpectedly Ellen lowered the Bible and looked around as if surprised to see everyone staring at her. "Oh—it's dark!" she exclaimed in her normal quiet voice. "Was—was I in vision a long time?"

"Yes, you were," Mr. Nichols said simply.

"God showed me a chain of truth in His Word that contradicts what Mr. Sargent and Mr. Robbins have been preaching," Ellen said solemnly. "He showed me that they will continue to despise the teaching of the Lord until they are left in total darkness and their foolishness is evident to everyone."

The meeting quickly broke up as everyone went home to ponder what they had witnessed. Mr. Nichols was even more convinced that Ellen's visions were from God—especially when Ellen's prediction came true. The teachings of Mr. Sargent and Mr. Robbins became even more extreme. They claimed to be free from sin, even while committing shameful acts. Within a year or two, their group broke up, and some of

---

* We don't know exactly what texts Ellen read, but some of them were about God's judgment of the wicked.

the members abandoned their faith in God entirely.

Ellen's vision reminded all who heard it of the importance of relying on the Bible for truth. Throughout her ministry, Ellen always uplifted the Bible as God's inspired Word.

As God's messenger and a member of the remnant church, Ellen White manifested the gift of prophecy, always upholding the Bible as the standard by which teaching and experience must be tested.

Digging in the Word

1. True prophets are people who receive a message from God and speak on His behalf to people. In Bible times, God used all types of people. Jesus warned us of false prophets (Matthew 7:15). When believers want to know whether a prophet is from God, they refer to the "tests of a prophet." Read the following verses and list the criteria for the tests of a prophet: Isaiah 8:20; Deuteronomy 18:22; 1 John 4:1-3; Matthew 7:16, 17.
2. Read Numbers 12:6 and Hebrews 1:1. What do those verses say about prophets?
3. Unscramble the underlined word:
   Jehoshaphat stood and said, "Have faith in the LORD your God and you will be upheld; have faith in his prophets and you will be <u>ecsscslufu</u>" (2 Chronicles 20:20, NIV).
4. Read Amos 3:7. How do you feel about the future after reading this promise?

Belief Bonus: God promised that there would be prophets in the last days (see Joel 2:28 and Acts 2:17, 18). Seventh-day Adventists believe that Ellen G. White passed the tests of the prophet. Whenever she spoke of her ministry, she referred to herself as "God's messenger." She referred to her writings as a lesser light that the Lord had given to lead men and women to the greater light, the Bible.[1]

---

1. Ellen G. White, *Colporteur Ministry* (Mountain View, CA: Pacific Press®, 1953), 125.

Surrounded by Flames

By Leonard C. Lee

🌿 Faith Seed 19: The Law of God
The Ten Commandments show us how to love God and others.

When I was a small boy growing up in North Dakota, I often went out to the field to meet my father near quitting time. He would sometimes let me ride home on the plow or on one of the horses.

One afternoon I headed toward him, walking through the tall grass that had been partly trampled down by the horses going back and forth to the field. I saw my father driving a team of five black horses—two in front and three behind—pulling a double plow, the kind a driver rides on.

Then, suddenly the horses began to run—fast! They came straight toward me, and their hoofbeats sounded like thunder. I tried to run out of the pathway, but I didn't have time. Fortunately, the horses saw me and swung to one side to keep from running over me. Then, I spotted my father standing on the plow, swinging a long whip and shouting "whoa" at the horses. I gazed up into his scared face as the little furrow wheel almost hit me.

I fell down trying to get away from the plow, and before I could get up, I heard the horses coming back. They were still running—but not as fast. My father kicked the trip lever, and the plowshares hit the sod, sending dirt flying ten feet. This pulled the horses down to a trot.

They would have stopped, for the sod was heavy and tough, but my father swung his whip again, and they kept going. All around me, they plowed three double furrows and part of a fourth. Then my father stopped them and came and picked me up and set me on the plow while he lit a match and burned all the grass inside the ring he had plowed. He scratched a circle about four feet across right in the middle of the

83

burned area and, lifting me by the shoulders, put me in it.

"Stay right here till I come back!" he commanded. "Don't go out of this little circle."

He had done everything so quickly that I didn't dare ask why. I had never seen my father look like that or do things so fast.

Then he jumped on the plow, swung his whip, and shouted at the horses. They ran away, leaving me wondering, *Why did they go home without me?*

I didn't know it, but my father had seen a prairie fire that had been started by some careless person, and the wind was carrying it right toward our home. My mother and sister and little brother were there, and Father was hurrying home to try to save them and the house. We had no close neighbors, so Father knew it was up to him.

I wanted to follow him home, but I had been taught to obey. I had found out the hard way that when my father gave an order, he really meant it and I had better obey him. So I sat in my little circle and waited for him to come back.

Pretty soon, animals began coming into my circle. Several striped gophers scampered in and then a jackrabbit. Prairie chickens fluttered overhead, and other birds began flying over. Then I began to smell the acrid fumes of fire, and the air got heavy and full of smoke. A coyote came running into my circle. It took a good look at me and ran out the other side and away through the long grass toward the field my father had been plowing. A rabbit with its fur half burned off came into the circle and tried to crawl under me. I tried to push it away, but I couldn't.

The air got hot, and I wanted to run, but Father had said, "Stay till I come back," and I knew I had to stay. Then it got so hot that I could hardly stand it, but I had to try.

Fire came right up to the outside of the plowed furrows all around me, and the flames reached out like the arms of a giant trying to grab me. My clothes started to burn. I rolled on the ground and tried to dig into the burned sod, but it wasn't any use. The half-singed rabbit and I tried to hide behind each other.

Then I heard the thunder of the horses' hooves and knew that my father was returning. I tried to open my eyes, but my face was so blistered from the heat that only one eye would open a little bit. The team was coming right over the burning prairie. Their black coats were white with sweat and foam, and they were running as I have never seen horses run since that day. Father held the four lines in one hand and the whip in the other. The horses came right into the circle, but they didn't run over me.

My father tore off his shirt, wet with sweat, and wrapped it around me to put out the fire, for some of my clothes were smoldering from the heat. That is the last thing I remember, for I woke up at home in bed.

Father, with some help from the neighbors, had saved the house by plowing furrows in front of the fire and then backfiring. Then the wind had changed, and the fire had started going toward my refuge.

Father had turned the tired horses and lashed them into foaming furies in the wild ride to save my life. In his heart was the awful question *Has my son obeyed?* Life and death hung on that word *obey*.

I often think that I would not now be alive if I had not obeyed my father. And someday I will look back to the trials and dangers of this life and think, I would not have gained eternal life if I had not obeyed a loving God and Savior.

For I have learned from this experience that there is safety in obedience. Our heavenly Father is just as interested in our eternal safety as my father was in my earthly safety. If we will obey our heavenly Father perfectly, we will be safe.

I like to hear a song called "God Leads Us Along," which contains these words: "Some through the waters, some through the flood, some through the fire, but all through the blood."

Leonard's father asked him to stay where he was, and because of his obedience, Leonard was safe. God gave us the Ten Commandments as an expression of His love, and there is safety in obeying them.

Digging in the Word

1. According to Matthew 5:17-20, what happened to God's law when Jesus came to the earth? How important is righteousness?
2. Read James 2:14-26; Mark 12:28-31; and John 14:15. How would you respond to a person who says, "The only thing that matters is that I love God. What I do doesn't matter"?
3. Who has sinned, and what provision has God made for those who have sinned? Romans 3:23; 8:3, 4

The Bull That Preached

By Rachel Whitaker Cabose

⬭ Faith Seed 20: The Sabbath

The Sabbath is the Creator's gift to us, a time for rest and
restoration that reminds us of God's Creation and Jesus' grace.

Pastor Timothy, I need your advice." Nathaniel's furrowed brow revealed his
concern. "The nurses from the Seventh-day Adventist hospital in Atoifi are holding a clinic here in Kwaibaita. You've often warned us about Adventists' misguided
doctrines. Is it safe to go to their clinic?"

Pastor Timothy thought carefully before replying. As a pastor and the paramount
chief of the entire Kwaibaita district, he was well respected by the people of his
community in the Solomon Islands.

"We do need medical care here in the village," he admitted. "You can accept the
Adventists' medications, but don't listen to their teachings. If they tell you anything
about the Bible or the church, just ignore it."

After Nathaniel left, Pastor Timothy felt a pang of guilt.

*In twenty years as a pastor, I've found some texts in the Bible that make me wonder if
the Adventists are right about some things. Take the fourth commandment, for example . . .*

He quickly shoved that thought out of his head. What would his church members
think if he suddenly changed his mind about Adventists and their teachings?

"We have a lot of work to do in the garden this morning," Pastor Timothy said
to his wife and their ten-year-old son, Bofanta, one September day in 1990. It was
a Sabbath morning, but that did not bother Pastor Timothy because he did not
believe that Saturday was the Sabbath. "The taro plot will be full of weeds after all
the rain we've had."

The three of them walked down the path away from the village. Pastor Timothy
paused to open the gate of the cow pasture they had to cross to reach their garden.

87

As they neared the other side of the enclosure, his wife spoke up. "Look at how all the cows have lined up facing us. It's almost as if they're trying to block our way."

"They look like soldiers on parade," Pastor Timothy said with a laugh. "I suppose they'll move when we get closer."

But the cows didn't move. *Odd*, he thought. *I guess we'll have to go around them.*

At the end of the line stood a large, muscular bull that seemed to be staring straight at them. As the family approached, the bull suddenly spoke in the Kwaibaita language. "Why are you going to the garden now? Don't you know that today is the seventh day, the Sabbath of the Lord God?"

Pastor Timothy's jaw dropped. "Did you hear that?" he croaked to his wife.

"I-I think the bull just talked!" she whispered hoarsely.

Pastor Timothy looked around, certain that he must have been mistaken. No one else was in sight.

Then he heard the voice again. "Timothy!" His head swiveled toward the bull. "Timothy, I'm speaking to you!"

Yes, the sound was coming from the animal. Its mouth was even moving as it talked.

"Th-there must be a devil in you to make you talk like that," Pastor Timothy said, his voice trembling.

"I am not the devil," the bull replied. "I am the voice of Jesus talking to you."

Pastor Timothy really paid attention then! The bull went on: "Today is the Sabbath of God. Don't you know that God gave you six days to work, and the seventh day is the Sabbath? You have been a pastor, and yet you don't know these things? How blind can you be?"

He's right, Pastor Timothy thought. *I've been refusing to believe the truth all this time.*

But the bull was not finished. "You must not work in your garden today. Go home and read Jeremiah one, verse 5. Share it with your people. Then look for the Seventh-day Adventist pastor, Pastor Bata. He will further explain these things to you."

Pastor Timothy waited, but the bull said nothing more. The pastor dropped to his knees in the field and began to cry. "I'm supposed to be a spiritual leader," he moaned, "but instead, I've been teaching my church members the wrong things! I'm sorry, Lord."

The pastor and his family immediately headed back to their house, taro plants and weeds forgotten.

"I must look up the text the bull mentioned," Pastor Timothy said when they reached home. He found the passage in his Bible and read it aloud: " 'Before I formed you in the womb I knew you, before you were born I set you apart; I appointed you as a prophet to the nations' [Jeremiah 1:5, NIV]."

"What does that have to do with the Sabbath?" Bofanta asked.

"I think God is saying that I need to share this message with others," his father replied.

Pastor Timothy called the entire village together and told them what had happened. "It was the voice of Jesus that spoke to me through the bull," he said. "We must not do any work today. We must begin resting on the Sabbath."

The people stared at him in amazement. But they respected their pastor and chief, so everyone in the village kept that Sabbath.

Early the next morning, Pastor Timothy set off through the bush toward Atoifi Adventist Hospital. Questions rushed through his mind as he walked along the steep, rocky mountain trail. There were so many things he needed to ask the Adventist pastor!

After a four-hour hike through the lush tropical forest, he reached the hospital and approached the first employee he saw.

"My name is Timothy, and I'm the chief of Kwaibaita," he said. "I am looking for Pastor Bata."

"Who told you about Pastor Bata?" the puzzled employee asked.

Pastor Timothy didn't answer the question directly.

"I have a story to tell Pastor Bata," he said.

Someone took him to the village where Pastor Bata was working. "I've already kept the Sabbath," Pastor Timothy told him. "I need to know more."

The two pastors studied the Bible together for three months. "I want to be baptized," Pastor Timothy decided. "And I want to do it in my village so that all my people can see the choice I'm making."

Pastor Timothy's baptism was a big event in Kwaibaita. Most of his church members showed up to see the man who had warned them against Adventism become an Adventist himself.

"For many years, I taught you things that I knew were not according to the Bible," Pastor Timothy confessed. "I ask your forgiveness for leading you astray."

He looked out over the crowd, full of people he cared about. "I've shared with you many of the things I've learned from the Adventist pastor. I believe them to be the truth. Will you join me in following God's Word? If you will join me, come stand over here to my right. If you want to stay with your current beliefs, stand on my left."

For a moment, no one moved. Then several people jumped up and strode purposefully toward Pastor Timothy's right. A few, with looks of horror on their faces, headed in the opposite direction.

As more and more people in the crowd chose one side or the other, Pastor Timothy's face broke into a broad smile. The majority of the villagers were taking their stand with him to follow God's truth!

Soon a new church was built in Kwaibaita where Pastor Timothy and his people could worship God every Sabbath.

And the talking bull? He hasn't said a word since. He doesn't need to. He lets Pastor Timothy do all the preaching about the Sabbath.

———————————

Bible-reading Christians don't need to wait for a bull to tell them that the seventh day is the Sabbath. The fourth commandment says it clearly.

Digging in the Word

1. Who rested on the first Sabbath? Genesis 2:2
2. Exodus 20:8–11 invites us to keep the Sabbath. How would your life be different without Sabbath rest? If you don't rest on the Sabbath, how might resting on the Sabbath change your life?
3. What did Jesus routinely do when He was on the earth? Luke 4:16
4. What will all flesh (all people) do throughout eternity on Sabbath? Isaiah 66:23

The Mystery of the Missing Tithe

By Troy Smith

🌱 Faith Seed 21: Stewardship

God blesses us for being responsible with the good things He gives us.

I burst into the house all excited. "Mom, look! Mrs. Burns paid me for mowing her lawn and cleaning out her flower beds!"

"That's good, Son." Mom smiled. "You've been helping her on Sundays for the last month or so, and I'm glad she gave you some money for it. I know you'll tithe it first."

I looked at Mom, and my smile got smaller. But I said, "Sure, Mom. I made twenty dollars, so I guess I'll give God two dollars for tithe and maybe fifty cents for offering."

As I dashed upstairs, I ran into my sister, Kim. "Hey, Thomas, look out! You're going so fast you almost made me drop my picture frame!"

"Oh, sorry, Sis. Hey, look, I need one of those tithe things Dad has in his coat pocket. I'm going to tithe in church on Sabbath."

"I guess Mrs. Burns paid you and you've got money," Kim said with a grin.

"Yeah, she did, and Mom said I tithe first before I spend my money on other things."

Just then I heard the door slam. It was Dad coming home, so I decided to get the tithe envelope directly from him. He looked tired, so I waited until after dinner to ask him about the tithe envelope. "Sure, Son," he said. "I have one in my coat pocket. I'm glad you're putting God first. Do you know how to fill it out?"

"Yeah, Dad. I've seen you do it before, and I did it when I got money on my tenth birthday." I took the envelope and filled it out. Then I put it in the inside pocket of my suit jacket, all ready for Sabbath.

What We Believe

On Sabbath I woke up feeling extra cheerful. I got dressed and made sure I had my tithe envelope in my suit jacket.

When Kim saw me, she said, "Thomas, make sure you put your tithe in when it's time for offering."

"Don't worry, Sis. I have it under control," I assured her.

After Sabbath School, I walked with my friend Caleb toward the pew where my parents were seated. "Thomas, sit with me and Landon in the back so we can make paper airplanes," Caleb urged. "Church is long sometimes."

"Not today," I said. "My mom always looks for me, and besides, I don't want to get in trouble." As I was walking toward my seat, I checked my inside pocket. My tithe was gone! I hunted through all my pockets for the envelope but didn't find it. Finally I sat down next to Mom. My worry must have shown on my face.

"What's the matter, Thomas?" Mom asked.

"Um, nothing, Mom. I'm OK," I replied, even though it wasn't exactly true.

I kept fidgeting around, trying to find my tithe, but it wasn't in my jacket. I didn't know where I had dropped it, and I didn't want to tell Mom or Dad.

Kim poked me. "What's up with you, Thomas? Calm down."

I tried to be still, but during prayer time I took another tithe envelope, sealed it, and put it in my Bible. During tithes-and-offering time, when the deacons began passing the plates, I put the empty tithe envelope in the plate. What else was I going to do? Everybody was looking at me, and I didn't want to let my mom and dad down. So I put the envelope in and sat back.

After church I saw Caleb. "Did you see a tithe envelope in our Sabbath School class?" I asked him. "My tithe envelope disappeared, and I thought maybe I dropped it there."

Caleb shook his head. "No, I didn't see anything, but you need to tell a deacon. Maybe someone stole it."

"I don't think so," I said. "Who would steal money in a church?" But now I was even more puzzled.

During the drive home I was quiet. *I don't think I did anything wrong,* I argued with myself. *Besides, I didn't put my name on the empty envelope, so nobody will know that I was the one who put it in the offering plate.*

At lunch I didn't eat much. As soon as the meal was over, I went to my room. Kim followed me.

The Mystery of the Missing Tithe

"Kim, I want to take a nap. Leave me alone."

"What's wrong, Thomas?" she asked. "You've been edgy all day. What's going on? Tell me. I'm your big sister—I might be able to help you."

I sighed. "I don't think you can help me this time, Sis. I lost my tithe, and I—"

"Hey, wait a minute. We all saw you put your tithe in the offering plate. What do you mean, you lost it?"

"It was an empty envelope, Kim. I just did that so everybody would think that I'd put my tithe in the plate. But really I lost the money."

Kim gave me a comforting pat on the shoulder. "Oh, Thomas, it's God's money, and I'm sure if He needs you to find it, He'll work it out. But you need to tell Dad what happened. And praying about it wouldn't be a bad idea either."

The next day was Sunday, and my dad was working outside when I came up to him. "Dad, I need to talk to you about something."

"OK, Son. Here, take this rake, and let's sit down under the tree. You look serious. What going on?"

"You know that Bible text that says, 'God loves a cheerful giver' [2 Corinthians 9:7]?"

"Yes, Son. What about it?"

"Well, I'm not very cheerful. I lost my tithe envelope, and I didn't know what to do, so I put an empty one in the plate. Everybody was looking at me, so I just did it."

I put my head down and closed my eyes. Then I felt Dad's arms around me. "It's OK, Son. Your heart was in the right place. But next time tell me or your mother. Anyway, I'm sure someone will find your tithe and put it in later."

I felt a lot better after that—but I still wondered whether my tithe would ever make it into God's treasury.

That summer I worked some more for Mrs. Burns, and when she paid me, I did return my tithe. But I still didn't know what had happened to the $2.50 that I had put into the tithe envelope months earlier.

Then one Sabbath, the pastor came up to me after the service. "Thomas Williams," he said.

"Yes, Pastor."

"One of our workers found this behind the old water fountain." The pastor held out a stained tithe envelope. "We got a new water fountain, and when the worker was taking out the old one, he saw this stuck behind it. Look—it has money in it, and your name is still on it, even though it got wet and dried out so many times."

I took the envelope from his hands in amazement. "Oh, thank you, Pastor! I wondered what had happened to it."

I hurried to show my sister. "Look, Kim! The pastor gave me my old tithe envelope! It must have fallen out of my coat pocket when I bent down to get a drink from that old water fountain. It sat so low you practically had to do a headstand to drink out of it."

Kim grinned. "That's great, Thomas! Now what are you going to do?"

I grinned back at her. "I'll put it in the offering plate next week—for real!" I paused as I tucked the envelope away very carefully. "And I think I'll also bring a thank offering!"

God has given us resources for which we are responsible. When we return 10 percent of our resources to God, we are recognizing that God is the one who gave them to us. This is often referred to as tithing.

Digging in the Word

1. Stewardship is taking care of something that doesn't belong to us. What resources has God given you to be responsible for?
2. Who asked people to take care of the world, and what are some reasons for the believer to be a good steward? Genesis 1:26-28; 2:15; 1 Chronicles 29:14; Colossians 3:23
3. Read Malachi 3:8-12. Have you experienced the blessings of faithfully returning tithe and offering? If not, what is keeping you from doing so?
4. What should our attitude be when we give to the Lord? 2 Corinthians 9:7

Belief Bonus: The Bible was originally written in Greek and Hebrew. The word *tithe* in Greek, *dekate*, and in Hebrew, *maaser*, mean a tenth part.[1]

---

1. Bible Hub, Topical, s.v. "baptizo" https://biblehub.com/topical/t/tithe.htm.

The Nightclub

By Rosanne Fortier

⌒ Faith Seed 22: Christian Behavior

God calls us to honor Him in mind, body, and spirit.

This road sure is dusty, I thought as I walked along with the group of girls, wondering if I should even be there. I knew my mother would figure out something if I wasn't home on time. My friends, along with my enemy, were taking me to a nightclub.

I had never been to a nightclub before, but I had heard that the music was good enough to give a person goose bumps. I was thirteen years old, and listening to music was one of my favorite pastimes, so I couldn't wait to get there.

My thoughts were interrupted by my friend Linda asking, "Are you sure they'll let us in? We're obviously not old enough."

Josie, whom I didn't like very much, put an angry smirk on her face. "Stop making a fuss. I know someone who will let us in," she answered.

I was glad she was so sure of herself because my feet were getting harder to move. We passed houses covered in cracked stucco with the strangest symbols painted on the walls. Mom had told me to be careful of certain places in the city. I had grown up on a farm and wasn't aware of all the dangers. My stomach tightened.

Yet, at the same time, there was a swing to my steps. A part of me craved adventure. The rest of me wanted to run inside a church or anyplace that was safer than here.

I spotted the light rail transit in the distance. After that, I saw only gas stations and dust blowing in circles. I couldn't imagine anything exciting happening around here.

Then I noticed that Josie was doing a little dance of excitement. "It's right over there. We're going to party," she called out.

Up ahead, I saw a square building with steel covering it. It didn't look like I thought it would. Nothing I'd seen so far had.

What We Believe

When we got to the nightclub, the woman whom Josie knew came to the door. Then a man with tattoos on his arms came up to the woman. "These are teenagers. We can't let them in," he told her.

She shook her head. "No, they just look young for their age."

His forehead wrinkled up and down, but we went inside anyhow. Lights of all colors danced on the ceiling. The music seemed to spark with electricity. It filled me with energy.

We found a seat. A waiter came and asked what we wanted. "I'll have an Orange Crush," I said.

Josie laughed. "I'll have a drink over here," she called out. The other girls said they would have the same thing as Josie.

When the waiter left, Josie turned to me. "If you think you're feeling good now, you have to try a drink."

"I don't think so," I muttered.

Josie swung her leg out. "What's wrong with you? Don't you want to be cool like us?" she said in a self-important tone.

"No, I want to take care of my body. My grandfather was an alcoholic. Nothing else mattered to him but his bottle of beer. He wrecked his life and his family too."

"Rosanne never wants to have any fun," Josie said in a sly tone. But the other girls were moving away too. That didn't bother me because the music was putting me into another world. But then the music stopped.

A man with a short, even haircut and an innocent expression came to our table and pulled back a chair. "I love the company of good-looking ladies like you," he said in a voice as smooth as peanut butter. "What college do you attend?"

He was looking directly at me, so I muttered, "Prince George."

His voice cracked as he replied, "I never heard of it."

Then I realized what I had done. I needed to tell the truth. "Actually," I said, "we don't go to college because we aren't eighteen yet."

He said something else that I didn't hear because a loud crash startled me. I looked around and saw a man who had helped my father when we used to farm. He was lying on the floor with blood pouring from his face. I suddenly remembered hearing his wife argue with him about his drinking.

When I looked more closely, I noticed that the cut was deep. I wondered if it would leave a scar.

Someone picked the man up and took him away. Then I realized that the man sitting with us was holding a bag of powder beneath the table. He whispered, "This will make you feel way out there. I won't charge you for it this time."

The other girls nodded. But I got up without saying anything. I could taste the tears dripping down into my mouth. But there was no fear left inside me as I walked home.

Mom never asked where I had gone.

The next day at school, no one talked to me–not even Linda. Weeks went by, and I still didn't have any friends. I went for a lot of walks during break times. Every day I went home by myself, and more tears dripped into my homework. Sometimes I wondered whether I had done the right thing.

One day I saw a poster hanging up in our church. It was for a Christian youth group. Their meeting was the following week. I decided to go.

At the youth group meeting, unfamiliar faces greeted me. My stomach sank. One girl said to me, "Let's get some of the drinks and refreshments over there." I hesitated until I saw the pastor's kind face. "Go ahead–you girls can help yourself," he said. They had apple, peach, and orange juices, as well as some dessert squares that looked like a circus full of colors.

We played a game of volleyball and watched a movie about Jesus. After that, they put on some Christian music. I kept thinking, *It feels so good just to be alive.*

I forgot about my lack of friends at school. Now I looked forward to the youth group.

One day as I was getting things from my locker at school, I realized that someone was behind me. It was Linda. She pointed to a poster I had made that hung in my locker. "That isn't bad," she commented.

"Thank you. I did it in my youth group. You can join, too, if you want. It's so much fun."

"I'll think about it," Linda said in a low tone.

I noticed that her expression was sad. "What's up?" I asked.

She stared downward as if memorizing the floor. "My uncle has cancer. They think it's due to his drinking," she said. "You were right with what you said about alcohol. I'm not going to drink again. My mom was so disappointed in me, and I felt awful the next day. I'm sorry I've been avoiding you."

I looked at Linda. Her eyes were still downcast. "That's OK," I said. "Let's go to the convenience store and get some Orange Crush. It will make us feel way out there."

We both laughed. It was good to be friends again.

Rosanne knew that her body was the temple of the Holy Spirit, and she took care of it by not consuming alcohol.

Digging in the Word

1. Fill in the blanks: Paul says our bodies are "the _____ of the _____ _____" and we are not our own. For we "were _____ at a price; therefore _____ God in your body and in your spirit, which are God's" (1 Corinthians 6:19, 20).
2. A person's behavior is carried out as a result of their thoughts. What does Paul say to the Philippians about thoughts? Philippians 4:8
3. Why should a Christian live a holy life? Romans 12:1; 2 Peter 3:11–14; 1 Thessalonians 4:7

Missionaries to Ohio

By Gary B. Swanson

🌱 Faith Seed 23: Marriage and the Family

A strong marriage between a man and a woman, along with a Christ-centered family life, helps children to grow up in security and love.

Dessa knew something was up—she just knew it!

Mom and Dad had been talking quietly together at times and stopped abruptly whenever she entered the room. One time she'd asked outright, "All right! What's going on?"

"Just talking," Dad had said with a shrug. But Mom had looked a little troubled.

"Is one of you sick?" Dessa asked.

Dad shook his head. "No, Dess, we're fine. We're just trying to work some things out, and soon we'll have something to share with you and Cam."

This had brought Dessa no real comfort. It had taken her longer than usual to fall asleep at bedtime for several nights. She lay there, staring into the darkness, as she tried to imagine what Mom and Dad were thinking about. It all scared her, and she'd prayed in a whisper, "Dear heavenly Father, You know what's going on with Mom and Dad. It feels as though something's wrong. Please bless and protect our family. And help me to put my faith and trust in You."

The next Sabbath afternoon, as they were finishing sliced watermelon for dessert, Cam, who usually finished first, rose to take his plate to the kitchen sink.

"Uh, wait a bit, Cam," Dad said. "We have something to talk about with you and Dess."

Here it comes! Dessa thought. *Cam probably hasn't even noticed anything at all!*

"For the past six years," Dad said, "Mom has enjoyed teaching her English classes at the community college. But she'd like to continue her own education and study for her doctorate. So we're going to be moving late this summer to Columbus, Ohio, where she'll be studying at a university there. This is going to be new for us, but we'll

work together to find our way through the changes."

Cam looked at Grover, their gray Manx cat, curled up in the sunlight in the kitchen corner. "What'll happen to Grover?" he asked.

Mom laughed. "Grover is part of the family. He will be going with us."

Dessa looked at her parents in disbelief. "Are you serious? I just graduated from eighth grade, and I'm going to the academy next year—with all my friends. What am I going to do in Columbus, Ohio?"

"We've thought about that, Dess. There's an Adventist school in Columbus. You will surely make friends there too."

"Hey," Cam said brightly, "it'll be like we're missionaries!"

Dessa shook her head. "No, it won't be like missionaries at all." She pushed back from the table and stalked down the hallway to her bedroom. "Perfect way to ruin a Sabbath afternoon," she muttered. "Finding out we're moving away!"

She flopped down on her bed and turned toward the wall, warm tears slipping from the corners of her eyes. "Dear heavenly Father," she prayed, "please don't let this happen! It just isn't fair!"

After a tap on her door, her dad came into the room and sat down on the chair by her desk. "We're sorry, Dess, but Mom and I have been praying about this. We believe that we've received some pretty strong signs that God wants Mom to finish her education."

"But what about me?" Dessa blurted. "Every friend I have is here in Fresno. How can I just leave and forget them?"

"You won't forget them, Dess. And you'll make some very good new friends in Ohio. It didn't sound like it just now, but after it sinks in, Cam is going to be scared too. Everyone in the family is concerned about the uncertainties—except maybe Grover, of course."

Dad smiled, but Dessa didn't. "That's the way you always deal with serious stuff, Dad. You try to be funny. This isn't funny."

Dad nodded. "I know, Dess. When I was a boy, Grandpa was in the military service. I attended four elementary schools and two high schools. It's tough having to move and make new friends. But I can tell you this for sure: our family stands together. And being a close, loving family, connected by God's love, will see us through."

The next morning, Sunday, was the one day of the week Dessa could sleep in. But something was going on outside her bedroom door. She could hear Cam whispering. "What's going on out there?" she growled.

The door creaked open, and Cam peeked in. "You awake?"

What We Believe

"I am now!"

"Cool!" he said. "I made this for you!" He elbowed the door open and brought a tray to the bed. "Fixed this to cheer you up."

Dessa didn't feel like it, but she sat up. Cam laid the tray clumsily in her lap.

"Who says I need cheering up?"

"I heard Mom and Dad talking about Ohio again. Dad said you're kind of mad about it."

Dessa looked at the tray, typical of her brother's idea of breakfast: a banana, two toaster pastries, and a glass of milk.

"You really did this all by yourself, didn't you?"

"Yep! How can you tell?"

"Let's just say it doesn't have Mom's nutritional touch."

Cam grinned. "Guess not. Can I ask a blessing on your breakfast?"

Dessa nodded her head slightly but smiled. "Sure."

"Dear Jesus," Cam prayed, "thank You for this breakfast this morning. Thank You for a good sleep last night. And, Jesus, we're kind of scared about moving to Ohio. Please help us to be brave and to go where You think it would be best for us—for our family. Amen."

Cam stood up and headed for the door. "See ya!"

"Hey," Dessa said, "hold on a minute. Yesterday all you could think of was whether we'd be leaving Grover behind. Now, today, you're scared?"

"Aren't you?"

"No! I mean, I guess, sure, the whole idea scares me. But it's more that I don't want to leave my friends."

"Oh, come on!" Cam said. "You make friends easier than I make breakfast."

Why am I having this discussion with a nine-year-old? Dessa thought with a sigh.

"Tell you what," she said. "When we're thinking about getting worried about this Ohio thing, let's get together and pray about it. In the meantime, you want to help me with one of these pastries?"

"Yeah, I can do that too!"

God created families to love and help each other. Dad and Cam fulfilled this purpose when they showed compassion and care for Dessa as she struggled to wrap her mind around a future move, which the family would make together for Mom's sake.

Digging in the Word

1. Who created the first family, and who were its members? Genesis 2:18–24
2. Read Exodus 20:12. (a) What promise accompanies the commandment to honor one's father and mother? (b) What do you think *honoring* means?
3. What does the Bible say about marriage in Matthew 19:3–9 and 2 Corinthians 6:14, NLT?

Night of No Return

By Derek Cyril Bowe

Faith Seed 24: Christ's Ministry in the Heavenly Sanctuary

God is getting ready to show the universe that He's handled the plan
of salvation—including everyone's choices—with love and fairness.

The words came at him hard and fast. Hiram Edson's neighbors in Port Gibson,
New York, peppered him with questions, taunts, and comments.

"Have you really not harvested your crops this fall?" a gruff voice asked
incredulously.

"That's right," Hiram started, smiling. "You see—"

"They'll rot in the fields!" a woman interrupted. "You and your family will starve!"
She dabbed at the tears beginning to slide down her cheeks.

A man took Hiram by the arm. "Brother Edson," he pleaded, "you've been a good
steady man all your life. Don't let your Second Coming views make a fool out of you!"

"That's right!" the crowd chorused, igniting a fresh eruption of insults.

"Preachers such as William Miller should be tarred and feathered!"

"Telling lies about Jesus coming to destroy the world on October 22!"

Hiram raised both hands, trying to quiet the crowd. Reluctantly the group
complied, the din subsiding until finally he was able to speak.

"Neighbors," Hiram began, "Brother Miller is no fanatical alarmist. Since 1816
he's studied the Bible, especially Daniel and Revelation, learning many new things.
He kept quiet about his discoveries, figuring he was a farmer and not a preacher. But
then he learned that the sanctuary is going to be cleansed in 1844, which propheti-
cally means that the world is going to be destroyed at that time!"

The crowd seemed to awaken, and Hiram hurried on. "Brother Miller knew
he had to tell people about their danger. That's why he's been preaching all over
New England for more than ten years. Jesus is coming in less than a week to

destroy the earth and take His followers home to heaven!"

Someone in the crowd gasped in fear.

"But there's still time to get ready," Hiram continued. "Come to Jesus in repentance and confession. Next week will be too late!"

Despite the man's heartfelt appeal, the crowd became infuriated.

"Who do you think you are?" they clamored. "You're no better than the rest of us!"

"What makes you think that millions of us—even our ministers--are wrong, and just the few of you Millerites are right?"

Hiram raised his hand again. "Friends," he said, "I see that you've made up your minds and that nothing I can say or do will–" Here his voice broke, and tears gushed down his face.

He looked over the crowd, from man to woman to child. These were people whom he had known for years. *How I love them!* he thought. *If only they would accept this truth and be saved!* But their minds were made up, and changing a New Englander's mind seemed to call for superhuman ability.

His trembling arms outstretched as though in blessing, Hiram managed to say, "May our God of love have mercy on you in His day of visitation."

"You're the one who will need mercy when Jesus doesn't come next week," someone retorted immediately. "I'll be at your home bright and early Wednesday to remind you of it!" Laughter swept over the crowd.

On that note, the group disbanded.

The sunrise on Tuesday, October 22, 1844, seemed the most glorious that the little group had ever seen. Amid clouds flecked with orange and yellowish hues, the sun came up triumphantly, chasing the shadows of the night away—just as Jesus would soon chase away the darkness of sin.

Huddled together in Hiram Edson's home, the believers had been up for hours. Who could sleep with such an event as Jesus' return about to explode on earth's stage?

All morning long as they gazed toward the eastern sky, they sang and prayed, prayed and sang, expecting at any moment to be interrupted by the trumpet announcing Jesus' arrival.

The sun climbed to its highest point. Still the little company praised God through prayer and testimony. Even when the sun began its westward descent, the group remained of good cheer. But as it dropped beneath the horizon, they struggled to keep their faith.

"Cast not away therefore your confidence, which hath great recompence of reward," Hiram encouraged, quoting Hebrews 10:35, KJV. "Our faith is being tested."

But night, dark and unrelenting, spread over the land. All too quickly, the clock struck midnight, and Jesus had not come back.

Dumbfounded, the Millerites stared at each other. Jesus had not returned!

First the children started whimpering, then burst into tears. Hugging them tightly, the women tried to comfort them, but their own tears and wails of lament joined the children's. The men rushed to soothe them all, but they too wept unashamedly. They all cried until it seemed they could cry no more. When the last tear was wiped away, it was Wednesday morning, October 23, 1844.

By daybreak, many of the group had returned home. When those remaining moved to the barn, Hiram tried to boost their spirits.

"Brothers and sisters, I don't know what has happened. But I do know that our God can be trusted." Heads nodded in agreement. Wiping his eyes, Hiram signaled everyone to kneel for prayer.

"Righteous Father, God of love, surely there must be some misunderstanding on our part as to why Your Son didn't come yesterday. Please reveal our error to us, and help us to be ready for the day He does return. In His name, amen."

"Brother Edson," someone said as they rose, "I'm confident that God has answered your prayer. But I'm concerned about the other Advent groups. Someone should encourage them too."

Immediately a young teacher, Brother O. R. L. Crosier, rested a hand on Hiram's shoulder. "Let's go at once, Brother Edson."

Hiram picked up his Bible and coat. "Let's go through the cornfields," he said. "Going along the road will bring us past our neighbors, and they've vowed to make fun of us."

At first, the two men walked side by side, picking their way past corn stubble. Neither spoke, so absorbed were they in their thoughts.

It was as bright a fall morning as New England had ever seen. The sun pierced the early morning mist with extra vigor, seeming to announce that everything would continue as usual on earth.

As Hiram considered these things, he walked slowly. Meanwhile, Brother Crosier picked up his pace, unaware that a large gap was developing between him and Hiram. Soon he was nearly beyond speaking distance.

"How long, O Lord," Hiram questioned, "must we remain in this world of sin?"

Suddenly something like an electric current coursed through Hiram's body, bringing him to a halt. He felt as though he were in the presence of God Himself. A conviction entered and then filled his mind. He could think of nothing else, even if he tried.

There *was* a reason for Jesus' "failed" appearance yesterday! Instead of coming to destroy the *earthly* sanctuary, He entered the *heavenly* one, beginning His work of cleansing it. When He finishes His high-priestly ministry there, He'll come to take His followers home to heaven!

"Praise God!" Hiram whispered in wonder. "God has answered our prayers!"

Just then, Brother Crosier turned around to say something to Hiram and was surprised to find him so far behind. "Why are you staying back there so long?" he shouted, thinking of the little groups that needed their comfort.

"God has answered our prayers!" Hiram said breathlessly, running up to him. "He's explained why He didn't come yesterday."

Brother Crosier listened as Hiram continued. "As you walked ahead, I prayed to understand what happened yesterday, and God answered. I felt an unshakable conviction that Jesus has entered the heavenly sanctuary to cleanse it of sin instead of coming to destroy the earthly sanctuary."

Crosier slowly smiled, regaining his composure. "That's good news, Brother Edson! Good news indeed!" Then he added with conviction, "But we'll have to search the Scriptures to see if it's really so."

True to their word, Hiram and Brother Crosier later met for Bible study. But the meeting was not just for a day. It stretched into several days—and sometimes nights! Another Advent believer joined the studies, the physician F. B. Hahn. Perseveringly the farmer, teacher, and doctor joined forces, humbly seeking the Holy Spirit's help to determine whether Hiram's revelation was from God.

Determined to let the Holy Spirit guide them, the men studied Bible verses such as Revelation 11:19 and Hebrews 8:2, which speak of a heavenly sanctuary. Slowly the pieces of the spiritual puzzle were falling into place.

"So there's a heavenly sanctuary in which Jesus functions very much like the Israelite high priest,"* Dr. Hahn said slowly, understanding the full meaning of Jesus' ministry. "In order to 'cleanse' the sanctuary as predicted in Daniel's prophecy, He has left the holy place and is now in the Most Holy Place, not offering an unblemished animal but presenting Himself as the perfect Lamb of God! He is showing once and for all that His sacrifice has completely taken away our sins."

---

* See Leviticus 16.

"And," Brother Crosier added, "everybody who accepts Him as Savior will be called His child and saved when He comes to the earth again after finishing His heavenly ministry."

"What a wonderful discovery!" exclaimed Dr. Hahn. "Let's thank God for helping us understand this important truth."

Together the men bowed as Hiram prayed. "Thank You, Lord, for the work You are doing in heaven right now to free us from sin. We don't know when You will come back to earth, but we trust that because of Your sacrifice, we will be ready when that glorious event takes place!"

Hiram Edson, William Miller, and many other Adventist pioneers believed that Jesus would return on October 22, 1844. They later came to an understanding that Jesus went into the Most Holy Place of the heavenly sanctuary to act as our Representative.

Digging in the Word

1. What does Jesus do in the heavenly sanctuary? Hebrews 8:1-6; 9:24-28
2. In the Old Testament sanctuary, sacrifices were performed regularly. How often did Jesus have to offer Himself as a sacrifice? Hebrews 10:10
3. What do believers need to do in order to be forgiven? Hebrews 10:19-22, NLT; 1 John 1:9

Zack and the Cloud

By Charles Mills

🍃 Faith Seed 25: The Second Coming of Christ

We look forward to Jesus' promised return. At that time, He will raise
from the grave those who've died believing in Him and take them,
along with all living believers, to heaven.

The first time he saw a tiny whiff of smoke, ten-year-old Zack should have stopped what he was doing and gone in and cleaned his room. But holding a magnifying glass over dried Tennessee grass was a lot more fun than picking up toys or sweeping dust under rugs.

Yes, he knew Grandma was coming. Yes, he knew his mother had told him to make his bed and remove any dirty clothes from his closet floor, and he'd do all those things very, very soon. But the magnifying glass he'd received for his birthday was such a cool tool that he just had to explore all the wonderful things it could do.

He'd already examined an ant, studied a leaf, and marveled at the beautiful design of the skin on his knee. He'd watched a worm dig in the soil and tried to catch a butterfly in the act of sucking nectar from a flower. Watching the worm had been easy. But the butterfly kept flying away.

Lacking anything new to examine, Zack had decided to try something he'd heard about from a friend. Seems a magnifying glass can focus sunlight to a tiny point that is hot enough to start a fire. He just had to check that out!

Feeling as if he were an explorer, Zack chose a deserted patch of land not far from the little country hospital where his dad worked as the administrator. He knew that, at this very moment, his father was sitting at his desk making important decisions that would help doctors and nurses do their work more efficiently. Zack loved his dad and enjoyed talking to him about all kinds of stuff, such as nature, God, and how birds can fly to South America without getting lost.

Zack bent low over the dried blades as the very bright point of light under the glass began to darken the side of a small sliver of wood. A tiny rill of smoke popped into view, followed by another puff. It was working. It was working!

Then, *POP!* The smoke turned into a tiny column of fire so hot and bright that it made Zack jump back in surprise. In seconds, the column grew in size and height, creating a very dark smoke that drifted with the gentle breezes blowing through the grasses. The boy reached out to extinguish the fire, but it was already igniting nearby stalks and creating a lot of heat.

Zack stood up, mouth open in surprise and shock. Maybe this hadn't been such a good idea. Maybe he should call someone. Maybe he shouldn't be here!

Mother saw her son burst into the apartment and hurry toward his bedroom. She was about to remind him that his room still needed cleaning when she heard shouts from outside. Walking to the window, she saw people running toward the little plot of land by the road between the apartment building and the hospital. The land was on fire! Flames lifted high into the afternoon air, and smoke was curling through the nearby trees. Some of the people were carrying buckets of water, while others were beating the hot blaze with blankets. In the distance, she heard the wail of an approaching fire truck. Mother was very glad that Zack was safe and sound in his room.

Uneasy feeling

That evening, after supper, Zack was sitting alone on his carefully made bed, feeling very uneasy. The fire had caused quite a stir in the neighborhood. Even students from the nearby Christian academy had come to help fight the blaze. Now, all that remained of his little "experiment" was a large, blackened area where there used to be grass, bushes, and flowers. Everyone was asking, "How did this happen? What started this fire?"

It could have been a lot worse. Just across the street sat the little country hospital filled with sick people who couldn't run from the flames if the fire had spread. Even his apartment building would have proved to be no match for a fast-moving brush fire. People could have gotten hurt, or even worse—all because he did something very foolish. He should've known better. He should've realized the danger. He should've—

"Zack?" The boy looked up to find his father standing in the doorway. "Zack, are you OK? You were so quiet during supper."

Zack shook his head. "Dad," he said quietly, "can I ask you something?"

"Sure."

Zack thought for a moment. "Remember how you said that God is coming soon, and we need to be ready to meet Him?"

"Yes."

"What if . . . what if you did something kinda bad, and then God comes, and He knows about it?"

Zack's father sat down beside his son. "Well, I think God would look at the situation carefully and—"

The man studied his child thoughtfully. "Zack," he said, "let me ask you a question. You know that Grandma is coming tomorrow, right?"

"Yes."

"And you've been busy cleaning your room—which looks great, by the way."

"Yes."

"Well, if Grandma would have come today before you'd finished cleaning your room, would she be unhappy to see you? Would she refuse to step into this room because there were still a few toys scattered about or because you hadn't finished straightening your closet?"

The boy shook his head slowly. "No."

"That's right. She would still be happy to see you because she knows you love her and couldn't wait to see her. Even if you had also done something bad, she would know that you were sorry and still loved her.

"Well, when we look up into the sky someday and see that little cloud coming from heaven—that cloud made up of angels with Jesus sitting on His golden throne—He'll be looking for all the people who truly love Him. Some will have already cleaned their rooms, and others will still be busy cleaning their rooms. He just needs to know that we truly want to be with Him forever and are doing our best to live the life He has told us is best for us. That's what's most important to Him."

A tiny tear slipped down Zack's cheek as he sat in silence beside his dad. He wanted to be ready for Jesus to come. He wanted to live with Him forever. Some days he would look up into the bright sky, searching for that tiny cloud, wondering when Jesus would return and, also, wondering whether he was ready to meet Him.

The boy stood to his feet and walked slowly across the room. Reaching into the top drawer of his dresser, he retrieved his magnifying glass. "I gotta tell you something, Dad," he said quietly. "I just want you to know that I'm very, very sorry."

Outside, as the sun was sinking behind the hills to the west, a tiny cloud drifted in the evening air. It wasn't Jesus and His angels. But if it had been, they would have found a little boy who wasn't perfect but who truly wanted Jesus to make him that way. That would have been exactly the type of person they were searching for.

Just as Zack prepared for his grandmother's visit, Adventists believe that Christians need to prepare for Jesus' soon return.

Digging in the Word

1. When will Jesus come back to the earth? Matthew 25:13
2. Who will see Jesus coming back? Revelation 1:7
3. How will He come back? Acts 1:9-11

A Promise of Tomorrow

By Kyla Steinkraus

🌱 Faith Seed 26: Death and Resurrection

People who've died believing in Jesus have nothing to fear in
death and will be raised up when He returns to the earth.

T hirteen-year-old Yumiko awoke groggy and aching. Her ribs felt bruised, and her
head pulsed with pain. Her eyelids fluttered open. Everything was white. The smell
of antiseptic and bleach filled her nostrils.

Her eyes focused on the beeping machine in the corner. She was in a hospital.

Yumiko sat up swiftly. The memories of the previous night flashed through her
mind like a horrible movie—she and her best friend, Taylor, riding in the car on their
way to Friday night vespers and singing loudly in the back seat while Taylor's father,
Pastor Mike, just shook his head.

And then the blaring headlights, the squealing tires, the bone-crushing crash—glass
shattering, metal crunching, Taylor's haunting scream . . .

"What—what happened?"

Her mother sat hunched next to the hospital bed. She squeezed Yumiko's hand.
"Last night a drunk driver swerved into your lane and struck your car head-on."

Yumiko touched her bandaged forehead, blanching. "My head . . ."

"You're OK, sweetheart. No broken bones. Just some cuts and bruises."

Yumiko looked around wildly, barely hearing her mother. "Taylor! Where's Taylor?"

Her mother's face crumpled. "Taylor went to sleep in Jesus last night, honey."

"No!" Yumiko cried. Grief washed over her in waves, filling her heart with
deep, wrenching pain. She couldn't even imagine the world without Taylor's
goofy smile. Yumiko wept for what felt like hours, her mother beside her, holding her hand.

"I'm so sorry, honey," her mother said after a while. "But, you have a visitor."

What We Believe

Taylor's father, Pastor Mike, shuffled into the hospital room. He had a broken arm and a cracked rib. But the pain in his eyes was far worse than his physical injuries.

"Aren't you angry at God?" Yumiko asked Pastor Mike. She'd lost her best friend, but Pastor Mike had lost his daughter. He had trusted God to keep her safe, but Taylor was still dead.

Pastor Mike shook his head wearily. "No, I'm not angry. I am sad and grieving, but as Christians, we don't grieve as the world grieves because we have hope."

"Why didn't God keep us safe?" Yumiko asked, tears streaming down her cheeks. "He knew that driver was drunk. He could have sent His angels to stop the truck, to keep that guy from ever getting in his truck in the first place."

"That is true," Pastor Mike said slowly. "We won't understand until heaven why God chooses to intervene in some situations but not others. But we know Taylor gave her heart to Jesus. God has saved her. For us, it is a long time to wait. But for God—and for Taylor—it will pass like the blink of an eye."

Yumiko nodded, her chin trembling. It was easier to understand with her head than her broken heart.

"Oh, honey," Mom said. There were tears in her own eyes. "Death is part of the fallen, sinful world we live in. But that isn't the way it is supposed to be. Our faith gives us hope that we will see Taylor again when the world is made new and sin is done away with, once for all."

Yumiko's raw and aching heart filled with longing. She imagined the day Taylor would rise from the grave when Jesus returns, and she and Yumiko could hug and laugh and sing and draw just as they used to.

"I have an idea," Yumiko said, sitting up straighter in the hospital bed. "There's something I want to do to honor Taylor."

After she'd asked permission from Pastor Mike and his wife, Yumiko called Taylor's friends from church—Mateo, Kali, and several others. She told them her plan.

Everyone agreed. On the morning of the funeral, Yumiko and five of Taylor's best friends arrived at the funeral home early. Yumiko had packed all of her gel pens and metallic markers, the ones she and Taylor had used so often, spending hours and hours doodling and drawing. She handed out Taylor's favorite colors—teal, rose-pink, tangerine, and plum-purple.

Silent tears splashed down Mateo's face. He scrubbed them away with his arm. "I'm sorry."

"Don't be," Yumiko said softly.

"Jesus wept at Lazarus' death, even though He knew He would raise Lazarus that very day. We will see Taylor soon, but it's still OK to be sad."

Solemnly, with red-rimmed eyes and determined faces, Taylor's friends went to work.

When they had finished, Yumiko stepped away from the coffin and examined their finished project. Scrawled in beautiful, brightly colored script across the inside of the coffin's lid, they had each written a message of hope:

"We love you, Taylor. Don't be afraid."

"Rejoice and be glad! You're about to see Jesus."

They all hoped that Taylor would see their handiwork when she awoke at the resurrection. But they knew there was the greatest possibility that the first thing she would lay her eyes on would be the loving face of her Lord and Savior.

This world held pain and sadness, but Yumiko clung to the promise that on the glorious day of Jesus' return, the dead in Christ would rise first—and her best friend would be among them.

Yumiko, her friends, and Taylor's family mourned Taylor's death, knowing that Taylor was sleeping in Jesus' arms until He returns and resurrects her. Like them, when our loved ones die, we can cry, knowing that there's hope and that Jesus will resurrect those who died having accepted Him as their personal Savior.

Digging in the Word

1. What happens to people when they die, and what do they know? Genesis 3:19; Ecclesiastes 9:5

2. Read 1 Thessalonians 4:13-17 and answer the following questions: (a) What is death compared to? (b) How should Christians grieve when compared to non-Christians? Why? (c) Why should believers be so sure that they will rise? See verse 14. (d) Do saved dead people go to heaven before Jesus' second coming?

3. When Jesus returns, what will happen to death? Revelation 21:4

4. What did demons do to people, and what did Jesus do to them? Matthew 8:16, ESV

5. Many people are fascinated by media that portrays demons and witches in a positive light. In the media we see people interacting with mediums and sorcerers and

trying to talk to their dead loved ones. Don't fall into Satan's trap! Read what the Bible has to say about the supernatural in Leviticus 20:6; Deuteronomy 18:10-13; Isaiah 8:19; and 2 Corinthians 11:14, 15. Imagine that someone invites you to play with a Ouija board or to watch a movie about a ghost or witch. How would you respond?

The Great Tootsie Roll Bank Robbery

By Rachel Whitaker Cabose

🍪 Faith Seed 27: The Millennium and the End of Sin

While the saved reconnect with God in heaven, Satan and his evil angels
are trapped on earth by themselves. After a thousand years, God will
resurrect the lost for the final judgment before destroying sin and sinners.

If our house had been messy, we probably wouldn't have noticed right away. But
my mom is a stickler for having everything in its place. So when our family came
home from a church member's funeral one day, it took just minutes for her to realize that something was wrong.

Walking into her bedroom, Mom noticed that the bedspread hung lopsided as
if someone had lifted it to look under the bed. *I didn't leave the bed looking that way!*
she thought.

Then she spotted one of the dresser drawers sticking out a few inches. Mom *never*
left dresser drawers open!

A chill ran down her back as she scanned the room to see if anything else was
amiss. "Joe," she called to my dad, trying to keep her voice even, "I think someone was
in the house while we were gone. Things have been moved around in the bedroom."

Dad hurried to her side. His eyes fell on the tray on the dresser, where he usually
kept spare coins from his pockets. "My change is gone!" he exclaimed. "I'm sure I
had some in there this morning."

Dad and Mom looked at the empty tray and then at each other. "Someone must
have broken into our house," Mom said, her voice edged with fear.

"I—I think you might be right," Dad responded. "I'll check around the house to
see if anything else has been disturbed. You tell the children what's going on." He
didn't voice the dreadful thought that had occurred to him: *What if the burglars are
still in here somewhere?*

Hesitantly Dad peeked into each room, half expecting someone to jump out.

Finding no obvious signs of a break-in on the main floor, he headed downstairs, his heart thumping louder with each step.

No criminals lurked in the basement, but in a dark corner above our old refrigerator, he spotted the telltale evidence: a hole where the small basement window was supposed to be. Our house had been burglarized!

Meanwhile, Mom rounded up my brothers and me and warned us that our home appeared to have become a crime scene. "Look in your rooms to see if anything is missing," she told us.

Dread rose in my heart as I headed down the hall. I had barely reached my bedroom when I heard a cry of alarm from my brothers' room. I rushed in to see my older brother, Jason, holding his coin bank, which looked like a giant Tootsie Roll.

"They took my money!" he cried. Sure enough, the bank, which had once jangled with coins, was empty. The lid and various trinkets that Jason had stuffed in the bank for safekeeping were strewn across his bed.

Now everybody was in a panic. My younger brother, Nathan, frantically pawed through his dresser, hunting for his matching Tootsie Roll bank. I dashed back to my room to see if my money was safe. My top dresser drawer was open, and my socks and shirts were tumbled about inside. I yanked open the next drawer and breathed a sigh of relief when I saw that the thieves had failed to find my coin bank.

I hurried back to the boys' room, where Nathan was almost in tears. "I can't find my bank anywhere," he wailed.

"Are you sure it was in your dresser?" Mom asked. "Look in the closet too." But a thorough search revealed no trace of the brown cardboard tube.

"They stole my money and my bank too!" Nathan stormed. "Grannie gave me that bank. I'll never be able to get another one!"

Shaken and scared, we huddled in the bedroom, mourning our loss. Sure, it wasn't a lot of money, but we didn't have much to begin with. We'd always felt safe in our country home. Now we knew that we weren't safe anywhere.

While Mom consoled my brothers, Dad called the sheriff's department to report the break-in. Soon an officer arrived to investigate. She dusted the basement refrigerator for fingerprints, assuming the thieves would have jumped down onto it after squeezing through the window. She walked around the outside of the house looking for clues and pointed out two sets of shoe tracks in the soft sand outside our front door, where our porch was about to be built.

"Probably a couple of kids," she told us. "At least one of them had to be pretty small to climb in through that window."

What We Believe

The officer jotted notes on her report form. "About how much money was taken?" she asked. Dad consulted with my brothers and concluded it couldn't have been more than twenty dollars.

"And nothing else of value was stolen?"

"Not that we could find. We don't really have a lot worth stealing," my dad said with a wry grin.

"You're lucky they didn't trash your house," the officer said. "Sometimes burglars do that when they don't find what they want."

Then came the moment I was waiting for: the moment when the officer drew herself up to her full height and announced that she and her fellow officers would do all in their power to find the criminals and bring them to justice.

Except that's not what happened. "The chances are pretty slim that we'll catch these kids," the officer informed us. "If multiple break-ins had happened in the same neighborhood, we might have more to go on, but . . ."

Even though she didn't finish the sentence, I knew what she was thinking: *we're not going to launch a countywide criminal search over a few dollars in change and a Tootsie Roll bank.*

My heart plummeted to my shoes. The one and only time in my life that we'd needed the services of law enforcement, they couldn't help us! My brothers' faces grew even longer as they realized that they would probably never see their life savings again.

The officer was right. The burglars were never caught. The Tootsie Roll bank robbery remains an unsolved crime to this day.

Sometimes I wonder what happened to the kids who stole our money. Was that break-in the start of a long life of crime? Did they eventually end up in jail for some more serious offense?

I don't know. But there is Someone who knows: God. The Tootsie Roll bank robbers may never face the penalty for their crime on this earth, but the Bible assures me that someday God will judge everyone's secret deeds, both good and bad (see Ecclesiastes 12:14). Stealing violates God's Ten Commandments, and those who hold on to their sins will eventually be destroyed in the lake of fire.

But there's another possibility. Perhaps those petty burglars felt so guilty over stealing change from a kid's bank that they changed their ways. Maybe they confessed their sin to God, accepted His forgiveness, and chose to follow Jesus. If so, I'll get to meet them in heaven!

God wisely gives His people a thousand years in heaven (the millennium) after Jesus returns before the wicked are destroyed. It's a time when our questions will be answered, and we'll find out exactly why some people made it to heaven and others didn't.

The county sheriffs may not have been able to solve the Tootsie Roll bank robbery, but during the millennium, I'll learn everything I need to know to put my mind at ease for eternity.

Rachel and her family never knew who stole from them and what the thieves did with their stuff. But during the millennium, her family and others who are saved will find out what happened, and we will take part in judging the wicked dead.

Digging in the Word

1. The millennium refers to a prophetic period of time that will take place in the future (see Revelation 20:1-6). When does it begin, and what are the saints, the wicked, and Satan doing during this time? 1 Thessalonians 4:16; Revelation 20:1-6
2. What else happens in connection with the first resurrection? 1 Corinthians 15:51-53; 1 Thessalonians 4:15-17; Revelation 16:18-21
3. What will the saints be doing during the millennium? 1 Corinthians 6:2
4. What does the Bible say about unbelievers having a second chance to repent during the millennium? Revelation 20:5; 22:11, 12
5. What will happen after God destroys Satan? 2 Peter 3:13; Revelation 21:1-5

Journey to Freedom

By Elfriede Volk

⬦ Faith Seed 28: The New Earth

God will re-create our once-broken world,
and He will live with us forever.

Mother looked gaunt when she opened the door. Her eyes had dark rings under them, her cheeks were pale and sunken, and lines furrowed her face.

It was the war's fault. World War II had caused Mother's great distress. Dad had owned a successful fruit and vegetable business once, but as a foreigner living in Germany, he couldn't get a permit to buy gasoline, so his trucks sat idle, and the produce rotted. That's when Dad sent Freddy to Holland to live with our married sister, Emma.

But when Freddy used up all the rationed soap, Emma sent Freddy back home.

"Where's Dad?" Freddy asked.

"In Glogów, working in a Red Cross hospital, so he wouldn't get drafted by the Organization Todt."*

"And Jack and Charlie?"

"In the army."

"And the girls?"

"At school."

"But, it's Sabbath!"

"Those who don't send their children to school on Sabbath have them taken away and placed where they get so-called proper training and instruction."

"God help us!" Freddy exclaimed.

Mother sighed. "We have to move," she said wearily.

---

* A civil and military engineering organization in Nazi Germany notorious for using forced labor

"Why? Move where?"

"The government wants our place to train members of Hitler Youth. But where can we go? Only God knows."

Someone finally took pity on my mother and agreed to let her have one room. Mother moved in with the five younger children. Freddy helped but stayed in the shed.

Soon we moved again to another city, where Freddy was told to join the Hitler Youth. When he refused, two fellows grabbed him and pinned him down. Another shaved him bald while his partner stood ready to paint the top of his head red.

After this humiliation, Freddy hid in the nearby hills whenever the Hitler Youth met. While he was hiding, soldiers brought a cart to take us to the train station. We were evacuated to Czechoslovakia without him.

When the war was over, Dad came to take us home, but we arrived in the midst of a typhus epidemic, which our thirteen-year-old sister, Rachel, caught. The fever ravaged her body, her hair fell out, and her flesh wasted away.

Mother tended to her day and night, leaving our fourteen-year-old sister, Milly, to look after the rest of us. I followed her everywhere, crying for Mother and crying from hunger. I even tried to eat a discarded household sponge, thinking it was a slice of moldy bread.

Dad was forced to work on a farm planting crops. One day, nine-year-old Willy took a jacket to Dad but didn't return until after curfew. A soldier saw him and threw him against a wall, then put a gun to his head. Willy sank down, crying and praying, and though the soldier had orders to shoot, he let Willy go.

With the peace treaty, borders changed. Our home was now in Poland. Dad risked his life, sneaking into a train station at night and riding on top of a train, to go to the Dutch Embassy in Warsaw to plead for help to return to the Netherlands.

When we arrived in Holland, government officials put us in emergency housing on the harbor with other homeless people. After several weeks, Freddy joined us.

"Freddy!" Mother cried. "How'd you get here?"

"Walking."

"But how did you know we were here, and how did you survive?"

"Dad told Frau Mueller you were going to Holland, and she asked me to take a letter to her sister in the west. Her sister fed me and let me spend the night, then gave me a letter for another relative, and so on."

"How were you able to cross the borders without papers?" Dad asked.

"By hiding in the hay that a farmer was taking across."

Though we were Dutch, some people did not accept us, probably because, except for Dad, we spoke only German.

One day, eleven-year old Dave was running an errand when he dropped a coin down into a storm drain. Using all his strength, he lifted the heavy cast-iron grating and reached down to retrieve the money. He was just bringing his hand up again when a boy kicked the grating, and it crashed down. "Take that, you stupid German," he yelled. The grate crushed one finger and almost severed it.

"We're going to Canada," Dad decreed when he heard what had happened. "I want a better life than this for my children."

A pastor who knew English helped him place an ad in the *Canadian Messenger*, and an Adventist rancher agreed to sponsor us.

Canada was better than expected. It was spring, and flowers were blooming everywhere. Compared to the drab and dingy harbor area, it was a paradise. And so vast! It took five days to get from Quebec to Castlegar, British Columbia. The train wound its way through forests, past lakes as vast as oceans, and across prairies where deer bounded away and children waved in welcome. Then it climbed the Rocky Mountains with peaks that glistened with snow.

A reception committee was waiting in Castlegar. They greeted us with smiles and hugs.

Two weeks after we arrived, on Willy's sixteenth birthday, a car drove into our yard.

"Visitors!" Mother panicked. "I have no chairs and nothing to serve."

"They are bringing their own chairs!" I exclaimed.

We sat in the once-empty living room, smiling, talking with our hands (because we didn't know the language yet), and singing. After Dad and Willy had come in from the evening's milking, women came out of the kitchen, bearing plates loaded with food. The feast ended with a cake ablaze with sixteen candles.

"Blow!" the people urged Willy, who had never seen a birthday cake before.

"Like this!" a teenage girl crowed, demonstrating.

Then Willy understood, and everyone cheered as the candles were extinguished.

When the last of the guests finally left, we could hardly walk into the kitchen. It was filled with furniture and boxes piled high. The boxes contained food, dishes, household goods, and anything else we might need. The church members had worked together for more than a year, preparing these gifts to share.

Even nature showered us with its bounties. Not to be outdone by spring, summer brought wild strawberries, saskatoons, blackcaps, and a host of other berries. Fall was not far behind with hazelnuts, and pears and apples left on deserted homesteads.

There was only one thing that troubled me. We'd have to start school in September. What would the teacher say when he found out we would not attend on Sabbath?

With my pounding heart, I approached Mr. Smailoff that first Friday.

"I will tomorrow not at school be," I told him in my broken English.

He stared at me.

"Tomorrow I go church," I explained.

"But, in Canada no one goes to school on Saturday," he said. "So you go to church tomorrow, I go on Sunday, and on Monday we both go back to school."

As I ran home that afternoon, I could hardly see because of my tears. But they were tears of joy. Canada was better than I could have imagined.

———————————

Elfriede and her family left a war-torn country that was full of limitations and moved to a country that was peaceful. Canada exceeded her expectations, much like the new earth will be far beyond what we can imagine! When the redeemed arrive at the new earth, the great controversy will be ended, death and suffering will be no more, and they will reign with God forever in a perfect world.

Digging in the Word

1. Read Isaiah 35; 65:17-25, and Revelation 21. Draw a picture of what you think the new earth will look like.
2. Who will be with people in the new earth according to Revelation 21:3?
3. How often will we remember past things? Isaiah 65:17, NLV.
4. Who will reign in the new earth, and how long will that kingdom last? Revelation 11:15
5. Revelation 21 is summarized in this paragraph: "The great controversy is ended. Sin and sinners are no more. The entire universe is clean. One pulse of harmony and gladness beats through the vast creation. From Him who created all, flow life and light and gladness, throughout the realms of illimitable space. From the minutest atom to the greatest world, all things, animate and inanimate, in their unshadowed beauty and perfect joy, declare that God is love." In what Ellen White book is this paragraph found?

Answers for Digging in the Word

1. The Holy Scriptures, p. 13

(1) God inspired the Bible, and it can be used to learn doctrine, for reproof and correction, for instruction in righteousness, and to guide us on our path to heaven. (2) Truth can be found in God's Word. (3) The Bible is described as living, powerful, sharper than any two-edged sword, and "piercing even to the division of soul and spirit, and of joints and marrow, and is a discerner of the thought and intents of the heart" (Hebrews 4:12). It remains forever. (4) The Bible was written "to warn [those of] us who live at the end of the age" (1 Corinthians 10:11, NLT).

2. The Trinity, p. 17

(1) Genesis 1:26 refers to more than one. (2) Believers are baptized in the name of the Father and of the Son and of the Holy Spirit. (3) The Three Members of the Godhead were present at Jesus' baptism.

3. The Father, p. 22

(1) God is love. (2) God the Father. (3) God, who is worthy to receive glory and honor.

4. The Son, p. 24

(1) The Son of Man came to serve and be a ransom for many. He is true, the Son of God, and a High Priest who can sympathize with our weaknesses and was "in all points tempted as we are, yet without sin" (Hebrews 4:15). (2) He suffered on our behalf and died for our sins, was buried, and resurrected. (3) Jesus was not proud.

5. The Holy Spirit, p. 29

(1) A Helper, the Spirit of truth. (2) He teaches us and reminds us of Jesus' words. (3) He would "convict the world of sin, and of righteousness, and of judgment" (John 16:8). (4) They would receive power and be witnesses to Him around the world.

(5) He "helps us in our weakness. . . . The Holy Spirit prays for us with groanings that cannot be expressed in words" (Romans 8:26, NLT).

6. Creation, p. 32

(1) God. (2) Six days. (3) Human beings.

7. The Nature of Humanity, p. 36

(1) Adam and Eve would surely die. (2) He was born a sinner. (3) The heart is deceitful and desperately wicked. (4) God has reconciled us with Himself through Jesus. (5) God asks us to love Him with all our heart, soul, mind, and strength; love our neighbor as ourselves; and take care of the environment.

8. The Great Controversy, p. 42

(1) The serpent, the great dragon, also known as the devil and Satan, introduced sin to the earth. (2) The conflict began in Lucifer's heart when he was in heaven. (3) Angels and men watch the great conflict. (4) A sinful life results in death. God offers us eternal life (Romans 6:23). (5) He gives you the Helper and the angels.

9. The Life, Death, and Resurrection of Christ, p. 46

(1) Answers will vary. (2) God sent His Son to save the world. Jesus lived a sinless life and wasn't a liar. (3) Jesus. He takes away the sin of the world. (4) God exalted Him, and now everyone in heaven and on earth and under the earth should confess (recognize) that Jesus is Lord.

10. The Experience of Salvation, p. 50

(1) Confess, repent. (2) He remembers His followers' sins no more. He removes our transgressions from us as far as the east is from the west. He forgives us of our sins and cleanses us from all unrighteousness. (3) Answers will vary. (4) Answers will vary. (5) God gives us a new heart and puts a new spirit within us. He takes the heart of stone out of our flesh and gives us hearts of flesh. He puts His Spirit within us and causes us to walk in His statutes, and we will keep His judgments and do them. He rescues us from darkness and transfers us into His kingdom. (6) We can know and memorize Scripture and let God put His law in our hearts. (7) Answers will vary.

11. Growing in Christ, p. 56

(1) Answers will vary. (2) Answers will vary. (3) They have authority over the power of the enemy.

12. The Church, p. 59

(1) "Christ is <u>head</u> of the <u>church</u>; and He is the <u>Savior</u> of the <u>body</u>" (Ephesians 5:23). (2) The church is "a chosen generation, a royal priesthood, a holy nation, His own special people," that they "may proclaim the praises of Him who called [them] out of darkness into His marvelous light" (1 Peter 2:9). (3) "Let's keep a firm grip on the <u>promises</u> that keep us going. [God] always keeps his word. Let's see how inventive we can be in <u>encouraging</u> <u>love</u> and <u>helping</u> <u>out</u>, not avoiding <u>worshiping</u> <u>together</u> as some do but spurring each other on, especially as we see the big Day approaching" (Hebrews 10:24, 25, *The Message*).

13. The Remnant and Its Mission, p. 63

(1) The remnant "keep the commandments of God and the faith of Jesus" (Revelation 14:12). (2) Be a worldwide witness. (3) Come out of Babylon.

14. Unity in the Body of Christ, p. 67

(1) Answers will vary. (2) When the church is united, it is following Jesus' example of being united with the Father. (3) Answers will vary. (4) Christians are united because of the shared mission and the hope of Jesus' return. We have been reconciled with God, and through our faith in Jesus, there are no more hierarchies or differences between us. We are all heirs of the promise through Jesus.

15. Baptism, p. 70

(1) John baptized Jesus by submerging Him. It is meaningful because Jesus is our ultimate Example of Christian living. (2) The sinner needs to repent. (3) Baptism symbolizes that we were buried (died to our sins) and raised to a new life in Christ through baptism. (4) Being fully submerged is important because being submerged in water symbolizes being buried, and coming out of the water symbolizes being raised to a new life.

16. The Lord's Supper, p. 74

(1) Answers will vary. (2) During the last supper Jesus used <u>bread</u> to symbolize his <u>body</u> and <u>grape</u> <u>juice</u> to symbolize His <u>blood</u> (Matthew 26:26–28). (3) Jesus promises

that the person who eats the bread of life will live forever. (4) They proclaim the Lord's death until He comes. (5) Before taking Communion, Christians should examine themselves and reconcile with others.

17. Spiritual Gifts and Ministries, p. 77

(1) (a) They distributed responsibilities among people other than the disciples so that people's physical and spiritual needs were met without burdening anyone. (b) Paul compares the church to a body because there are many different members who work together in different functions. (2) The Holy Spirit decides who gets spiritual gifts and gives them so that we can help each other. (3) Answers will vary.

18. The Gift of Prophecy, p. 82

(1) What true prophets say must agree with God's Word. Their prophecies must be fulfilled, they must confess that Jesus has come in the flesh, they will live in accordance with God's Word, and their ministry will have positive results (produce "good fruit"). (2) God will make visions known to a prophet and speak to him in dreams. God spoke through them at various times and in various ways. (3) Successful. (4) Answers will vary.

19. The Law of God, p. 86

(1) Jesus did not abolish the law; He came to fulfill it. In verse 20, Jesus emphasizes how much He values righteousness. (2) Possible answers: When a person truly believes, they live out their faith. If they don't, then they have no faith. It is equally as important to love God as it is to love our neighbor. A believer can't live Christianity in isolation. If we love God, we must keep His commandments. (3) All have sinned. God sent His Son.

20. The Sabbath, p. 90

(1) God rested. (2) Answers will vary. (3) He made it a custom to go to the synagogue on the Sabbath day. (4) All people will worship God from one Sabbath to another.

21. Stewardship, p. 94

(1) Some possible answers: money, time, nature, and our bodies. (2) God put us in charge of taking care of the world. We should be motivated by the fact that we were made in God's image. Everything we own has come from God, and He's asked us to do things as if we were doing them for Him. (3) Answers will vary. (4) We should be cheerful when we give.

22. Christian Behavior, p. 98

(1) Our bodies are "the <u>temple</u> of the <u>Holy</u> <u>Spirit</u>." For we "were <u>bought</u> at a price; therefore <u>glorify</u> God in your body and in your spirit, which are God's" (1 Corinthians 6:19, 20). (2) We should think about things that are true, noble, just, pure, lovely, of good report, have virtue, and are praiseworthy. (3) We should live our lives as "a living sacrifice, holy, acceptable to God, which is [our] reasonable service" (Romans 12:1). Our lives should be lived in holy conduct and godliness in anticipation of a new heaven and a new earth. God called us not to uncleanness but holiness.

23. Marriage and the Family, p. 103

(1) God created the first family, which was Adam and Eve (man and woman). (2) (a)The promise "that your days may be long" accompanies the fifth commandment. (b) Answers may vary. (3) Man cannot undo what God has joined. Divorce was not a part of God's original plan. We shouldn't marry unbelievers.

24. Christ's Ministry in the Heavenly Sanctuary, p. 108

(1) Jesus is "seated at the right hand of the throne of the Majesty in the heavens" (Hebrews 8:1), serves as "Mediator of a better covenant" (verse 6), and offers Himself as High Priest for men "to put away sin by the sacrifice of Himself" (Hebrews 9:26). (2) Jesus offered Himself once and for all. (3) We need to go boldly into God's presence with sincere hearts and confess our sins.

25. The Second Coming of Christ, p. 112

(1) Nobody knows. (2) Everyone from all nations of the world will see Him, including those who pierced Him. (3) Jesus will come to the earth in a cloud, just as the disciples witnessed Him returning to heaven.

26. Death and Resurrection, p. 115

(1) They return to dust and know nothing. (2) (a) Death is compared to sleep. (b) Christians shouldn't mourn like non-Christians because Christians have hope in the resurrection. (c) They can be sure that they, too, will rise because Jesus resurrected. (d) No. The saved dead will rise when Jesus comes, and then all the saved will go to heaven. (3) It will be no more. (4) The demons oppressed people. Jesus cast them out. (5) Answers will vary.

27. The Millennium and the End of Sin, p. 121

(1) The millennium starts when Jesus comes back. The saints who are dead are resurrected and live and reign with Jesus, along with the saints who are still living. The wicked are dead, and Satan is bound to the empty earth. (2) The dead in Christ shall rise, and those who are still alive are caught up. The saints are changed. There will be lightning and thunder and a great earthquake. Islands and mountains will disappear. There will be a great hailstorm. (3) The saints will judge the world. (4) Unbelievers are dead during the millennium. They have no time to change their minds. They have already decided to be unjust and filthy. They don't get a second chance. (5) The righteous will dwell in His new creation. The first heaven and earth will pass away. The New Jerusalem will come down from heaven from God. God will be with His people, and they will be with Him. He will be their God, and they will be His people. God himself will wipe away every tear from their eyes; death, sorrow, pain, and crying will no longer exist.

28. The New Earth, p. 125

(1) Answers will vary. (2) God will be with people. (3) Never. (4) Christ will reign forever. (5) It is the final paragraph of *The Great Controversy*, page 678.

28 Fundamental Beliefs of Seventh-day Adventists

1. The Holy Scriptures

The Holy Scriptures, Old and New Testaments, are the written Word of God, given by divine inspiration. The inspired authors spoke and wrote as they were moved by the Holy Spirit. In this Word, God has committed to humanity the knowledge necessary for salvation. The Holy Scriptures are the supreme, authoritative, and the infallible revelation of His will. They are the standard of character, the test of experience, the definitive revealer of doctrines, and the trustworthy record of God's acts in history. (Ps. 119:105; Prov. 30:5, 6; Isa. 8:20; John 17:17; 1 Thess. 2:13; 2 Tim. 3:16, 17; Heb. 4:12; 2 Peter 1:20, 21.)[1]

2. The Trinity

There is one God: Father, Son, and Holy Spirit, a unity of three co-eternal Persons. God is immortal, all-powerful, all-knowing, above all, and ever present. He is infinite and beyond human comprehension, yet known through His self-revelation. God, who is love, is forever worthy of worship, adoration, and service by the whole creation. (Gen. 1:26; Deut. 6:4; Isa. 6:8; Matt. 28:19; John 3:16; 2 Cor. 1:21, 22; 13:14; Eph. 4:4-6; 1 Peter 1:2.)[2]

3. The Father

God the eternal Father is the Creator, Source, Sustainer, and Sovereign of all creation. He is just and holy, merciful and gracious, slow to anger, and abounding in steadfast love and faithfulness. The qualities and powers exhibited in the Son and the Holy Spirit are also those of the Father. (Gen. 1:1; Deut. 4:35; Ps. 110:1, 4; John 3:16; 14:9; 1 Cor. 15:28; 1 Tim. 1:17; 1 John 4:8; Rev. 4:11.)[3]

4. The Son

God the eternal Son became incarnate in Jesus Christ. Through Him all things were created, the character of God is revealed, the salvation of humanity is accomplished, and the world is judged. Forever truly God, He became also truly human, Jesus the Christ. He was conceived of the Holy Spirit and born of the virgin Mary. He lived and experienced temptation as a human being, but perfectly exemplified the righteousness and love of God. By His miracles He manifested God's power and was attested as God's promised Messiah. He suffered and died voluntarily on the cross for our sins and in our place, was raised from the dead, and ascended to heaven to minister in the heavenly sanctuary on our behalf. He will come again in glory for the final deliverance of His people and the restoration of all things. (Isa. 53:4-6; Dan. 9:25-27; Luke 1:35; John 1:1-3, 14; 5:22; 10:30; 14:1-3, 9, 13; Rom. 6:23; 1 Cor. 15:3, 4; 2 Cor. 3:18; 5:17-19; Phil. 2:5-11; Col. 1:15-19; Heb. 2:9-18; 8:1, 2.)[4]

5. The Holy Spirit

God the eternal Spirit was active with the Father and the Son in Creation, incarnation, and redemption. He is as much a person as are the Father and the Son. He inspired the writers of Scripture. He filled Christ's life with power. He draws and convicts human beings; and those who respond He renews and transforms into the image of God. Sent by the Father and the Son to be always with His children, He extends spiritual gifts to the church, empowers it to bear witness to Christ, and in harmony with the Scriptures leads it into all truth. (Gen. 1:1, 2; 2 Sam. 23:2; Ps. 51:11; Isa. 61:1; Luke 1:35; 4:18; John 14:16-18, 26; 15:26; 16:7-13; Acts 1:8; 5:3; 10:38; Rom. 5:5; 1 Cor. 12:7-11; 2 Cor. 3:18; 2 Peter 1:21.)[5]

6. Creation

God has revealed in Scripture the authentic and historical account of His creative activity. He created the universe, and in a recent six-day creation the Lord made "the heavens and the earth, the sea, and all that is in them" and rested on the seventh day. Thus He established the Sabbath as a perpetual memorial of the work He performed and completed during six literal days that together with the Sabbath constituted the same unit of time that we call a week today. The first man and woman were made in the image of God as the crowning work of Creation, given dominion over the world, and charged with responsibility to care for it. When the world was finished, it was "very good," declaring the glory of God. (Gen. 1; 2; 5; 11; Exod. 20:8-11; Ps. 19:1-6; 33:6, 9; 104; Isa. 45:12, 18; Acts 17:24; Col. 1:16; Heb. 1:2; 11:3; Rev. 10:6; 14:7.)[6]

7. The Nature of Humanity

Man and woman were made in the image of God with individuality, the power and freedom to think and to do. Though created free beings, each is an indivisible unity of body, mind, and spirit, dependent upon God for life and breath and all else. When our first parents disobeyed God, they denied their dependence upon Him and fell from their high position. The image of God in them was marred and they became subject to death. Their descendants share this fallen nature and its consequences. They are born with weaknesses and tendencies to evil. But God in Christ reconciled the world to Himself and by His Spirit restores in penitent mortals the image of their Maker. Created for the glory of God, they are called to love Him and one another, and to care for their environment. (Gen. 1:26-28; 2:7, 15; 3; Ps. 8:4-8; 51:5, 10; 58:3; Jer. 17:9; Acts 17:24-28; Rom. 5:12-17; 2 Cor. 5:19, 20; Eph. 2:3; 1 Thess. 5:23; 1 John 3:4; 4:7, 8, 11, 20.)[7]

8. The Great Controversy

All humanity is now involved in a great controversy between Christ and Satan regarding the character of God, His law, and His sovereignty over the universe. This conflict originated in heaven when a created being, endowed with freedom of choice, in self-exaltation became Satan, God's adversary, and led into rebellion a portion of the angels. He introduced the spirit of rebellion into this world when he led Adam and Eve into sin. This human sin resulted in the distortion of the image of God in humanity, the disordering of the created world, and its eventual devastation at the time of the global flood, as presented in the historical account of Genesis 1-11. Observed by the whole creation, this world became the arena of the universal conflict, out of which the God of love will ultimately be vindicated. To assist His people in this controversy, Christ sends the Holy Spirit and the loyal angels to guide, protect, and sustain them in the way of salvation. (Gen. 3; 6-8; Job 1:6-12; Isa. 14:12-14; Ezek. 28:12-18; Rom. 1:19-32; 3:4; 5:12-21; 8:19-22; 1 Cor. 4:9; Heb. 1:14; 1 Peter 5:8; 2 Peter 3:6; Rev. 12:4-9.)[8]

9. The Life, Death, and Resurrection of Christ

In Christ's life of perfect obedience to God's will, His suffering, death, and resurrection, God provided the only means of atonement for human sin, so that those who by faith accept this atonement may have eternal life, and the whole creation may better understand the infinite and holy love of the Creator. This perfect atonement vindicates the righteousness of God's law and the graciousness of His character; for it both condemns our sin and provides for our forgiveness. The death of Christ is substitutionary and expiatory, reconciling and transforming. The bodily resurrection of Christ proclaims God's triumph over the forces of evil, and for those who accept the atonement, assures their final victory over sin and death. It declares the Lordship of Jesus Christ, before whom every knee in heaven and on earth will bow. (Gen. 3:15; Ps. 22:1; Isa. 53; John 3:16; 14:30; Rom. 1:4; 3:25; 4:25; 8:3, 4; 1 Cor. 15:3, 4, 20-22; 2 Cor. 5:14, 15, 19-21; Phil. 2:6-11; Col. 2:15; 1 Peter 2:21, 22; 1 John 2:2; 4:10.)[9]

10. The Experience of Salvation

In infinite love and mercy God made Christ, who knew no sin, to be sin for us, so that in Him we might be made the righteousness of God. Led by the Holy Spirit, we sense our need, acknowledge our sinfulness, repent of our transgressions, and exercise faith in Jesus as Savior and Lord, Substitute and Example. This saving faith comes through the divine power of the Word and is the gift of God's grace. Through Christ we are justified, adopted as God's sons and daughters, and delivered from the lordship of sin. Through the Spirit we are born again and sanctified; the Spirit renews our minds, writes God's law of love in our hearts, and we are given the power to live a holy life. Abiding in Him, we become partakers of the divine nature and have the assurance of salvation now and in the judgment. (Gen. 3:15; Isa. 45:22; 53; Jer. 31:31-34; Ezek. 33:11; 36:25-27; Hab. 2:4; Mark 9:23, 24; John 3:3-8, 16; 16:8; Rom. 3:21-26; 5:6-10; 8:1-4, 14-17; 10:17; 12:2; 2 Cor. 5:17-21; Gal. 1:4; 3:13, 14, 26; 4:4-7; Eph. 2:4-10; Col. 1:13, 14; Titus 3:3-7; Heb. 8:7-12; 1 Peter 1:23; 2:21, 22; 2 Peter 1:3, 4; Rev. 13:8).[10]

11. Growing in Christ

By His death on the cross Jesus triumphed over the forces of evil. He who subjugated the demonic spirits during His earthly ministry has broken their power and made certain their ultimate doom. Jesus' victory gives us victory over the evil forces that still seek to control us, as we walk with Him in peace, joy, and assurance of His love. Now the Holy Spirit dwells within us and empowers us. Continually committed to Jesus as our Savior and Lord, we are set free from the burden of our past deeds. No longer do we live in the darkness, fear of evil powers, ignorance, and meaninglessness of our former way of life. In this new freedom in Jesus, we are called to grow into the likeness of His character, communing with Him daily in prayer, feeding on His Word, meditating on it and on His providence, singing His praises, gathering together for worship, and participating in the mission of the Church. We are also called to follow Christ's example by compassionately ministering to the physical, mental, social, emotional, and spiritual needs of humanity. As we give ourselves in loving service to those around us and in witnessing to His salvation, His constant presence with us through the Spirit transforms every moment and every task into a spiritual experience. (1 Chron. 29:11; Ps. 1:1, 2; 23:4; 77:11, 12; Matt. 20:25-28; 25:31-46; Luke 10:17-20; John 20:21; Rom. 8:38, 39; 2 Cor. 3:17, 18; Gal. 5:22-25; Eph. 5:19, 20; 6:12-18; Phil. 3:7-14; Col. 1:13, 14; 2:6, 14, 15; 1 Thess. 5:16-18, 23; Heb. 10:25; James 1:27; 2 Peter 2:9; 3:18; 1 John 4:4.)[11]

12. The Church

The church is the community of believers who confess Jesus Christ as Lord and Savior. In continuity with the people of God in Old Testament times, we are called out from the world; and we join together for worship, for fellowship, for instruction in the Word, for the celebration of the Lord's Supper, for service to humanity, and for the worldwide proclamation of the gospel. The church derives its authority from Christ, who is the incarnate Word revealed in the Scriptures. The church is God's family; adopted by Him as children, its members live on the basis of the new covenant. The church is the body of Christ, a community of faith of which Christ Himself is the Head. The church is the bride for whom Christ died that He might sanctify and cleanse her. At His return in triumph, He will present her to Himself a glorious church, the faithful of all the ages, the purchase of His blood, not having spot or wrinkle, but holy and without blemish. (Gen. 12:1-3; Exod. 19:3-7; Matt. 16:13-20; 18:18; 28:19, 20; Acts 2:38-42; 7:38; 1 Cor. 1:2; Eph. 1:22, 23; 2:19-22; 3:8-11; 5:23-27; Col. 1:17, 18; 1 Peter 2:9.)[12]

13. The Remnant and Its Mission

The universal church is composed of all who truly believe in Christ, but in the last days, a time of widespread apostasy, a remnant has been called out to keep the commandments of God and the faith of Jesus. This remnant announces the arrival of the judgment hour, proclaims salvation through Christ, and heralds the approach of His second advent. This proclamation is symbolized by the three angels of Revelation 14; it coincides with the work of judgment in heaven and results in a work of repentance and reform on earth. Every believer is called to have a personal part in this worldwide witness. (Dan. 7:9-14; Isa. 1:9; 11:11; Jer. 23:3; Micah 2:12; 2 Cor. 5:10; 1 Peter 1:16-19; 4:17; 2 Peter 3:10-14; Jude 3, 14; Rev. 12:17; 14:6-12; 18:1-4.)[13]

14. Unity in the Body of Christ

The church is one body with many members, called from every nation, kindred, tongue, and people. In Christ we are a new creation; distinctions of race, culture, learning, and nationality, and differences between high and low, rich and poor, male and female, must not be divisive among us. We are all equal in Christ, who by one Spirit has bonded us into one fellowship with Him and with one another; we are to serve and be served without partiality or reservation. Through the revelation of Jesus Christ in the Scriptures we share the same faith and hope, and reach out in one witness to all. This unity has its source in the oneness of the triune God, who has adopted us as His children. (Ps. 133:1; Matt. 28:19, 20; John 17:20-23; Acts 17:26, 27; Rom. 12:4, 5; 1 Cor. 12:12-14; 2 Cor. 5:16, 17; Gal. 3:27-29; Eph. 2:13-16; 4:3-6, 11-16; Col. 3:10-15.)[14]

15. Baptism

By baptism we confess our faith in the death and resurrection of Jesus Christ, and testify of our death to sin and of our purpose to walk in newness of life. Thus we acknowledge Christ as Lord and Savior, become His people, and are received as members by His church. Baptism is a symbol of our union with Christ, the forgiveness of our sins, and our reception of the Holy Spirit. It is by immersion in water and is contingent on an affirmation of faith in Jesus and evidence of repentance of sin. It follows instruction in the Holy Scriptures and acceptance of their teachings. (Matt. 28:19, 20; Acts 2:38; 16:30-33; 22:16; Rom. 6:1-6; Gal. 3:27; Col. 2:12, 13.)[15]

16. The Lord's Supper

The Lord's Supper is a participation in the emblems of the body and blood of Jesus as an expression of faith in Him, our Lord and Savior. In this experience of communion Christ is present to meet and strengthen His people. As we partake, we joyfully proclaim the Lord's death until He comes again. Preparation for the Supper includes self-examination, repentance, and confession. The Master ordained the service of foot washing to signify renewed cleansing, to express a willingness to serve one another in Christlike humility, and to unite our hearts in love. The communion service is open to all believing Christians. (Matt. 26:17-30; John 6:48-63; 13:1-17; 1 Cor. 10:16, 17; 11:23-30; Rev. 3:20.)[16]

17. Spiritual Gifts and Ministries

God bestows upon all members of His church in every age spiritual gifts that each member is to employ in loving ministry for the common good of the church and of humanity. Given by the agency of the Holy Spirit, who apportions to each member as He wills, the gifts provide all abilities and ministries needed by the church to fulfill its divinely ordained functions. According to the Scriptures, these gifts include such ministries as faith, healing, prophecy, proclamation, teaching, administration, reconciliation, compassion, and self-sacrificing service and charity for the help and encouragement of people. Some members are called of God and endowed by the Spirit for functions recognized by the church in pastoral, evangelistic, and teaching ministries particularly needed to equip the members for service, to build up the church to spiritual maturity, and to foster unity of the faith and knowledge of God. When members employ these spiritual gifts as faithful stewards of God's varied grace, the church is protected from the destructive influence of false doctrine, grows with a growth that is from God, and is built up in faith and love. (Acts 6:1-7; Rom. 12:4-8; 1 Cor. 12:7-11, 27, 28; Eph. 4:8, 11-16; 1 Tim. 3:1-13; 1 Peter 4:10, 11.)[17]

18. The Gift of Prophecy

The Scriptures testify that one of the gifts of the Holy Spirit is prophecy. This gift is an identifying mark of the remnant church and we believe it was manifested in the ministry of Ellen G. White. Her writings speak with prophetic authority and provide comfort, guidance, instruction, and correction to the church. They also make clear that the Bible is the standard by which all teaching and experience must be tested. (Num. 12:6; 2 Chron. 20:20; Amos 3:7; Joel 2:28, 29; Acts 2:14-21; 2 Tim. 3:16, 17; Heb. 1:1-3; Rev. 12:17; 19:10; 22:8, 9.)[18]

19. The Law of God

The great principles of God's law are embodied in the Ten Commandments and exemplified in the life of Christ. They express God's love, will, and purposes concerning human conduct and relationships and are binding upon all people in every age. These precepts are the basis of God's covenant with His people and the standard in God's judgment. Through the agency of the Holy Spirit they point out sin and awaken a sense of need for a Savior. Salvation is all of grace and not of works, and its fruit is obedience to the Commandments. This obedience develops Christian character and results in a sense of well-being. It is evidence of our love for the Lord and our concern for our fellow human beings. The obedience of faith demonstrates the power of Christ to transform lives and therefore strengthens Christian witness. (Exod. 20:1-17; Deut. 28:1-14; Ps. 19:7-14; 40:7, 8; Matt. 5:17-20; 22:36-40; John 14:15; 15:7-10; Rom. 8:3, 4; Eph. 2:8-10; Heb. 8:8-10; 1 John 2:3; 5:3; Rev. 12:17; 14:12.)[19]

20. The Sabbath

The gracious Creator, after the six days of Creation, rested on the seventh day and instituted the Sabbath for all people as a memorial of Creation. The fourth commandment of God's unchangeable law requires the observance of this seventh-day Sabbath as the day of rest, worship, and ministry in harmony with the teaching and practice of Jesus, the Lord of the Sabbath. The Sabbath is a day of delightful communion with God and one another. It is a symbol of our redemption in Christ, a sign of our sanctification, a token of our allegiance, and a foretaste of our eternal future in God's kingdom. The Sabbath is God's perpetual sign of His eternal covenant between Him and His people. Joyful observance of this holy time from evening to evening, sunset to sunset, is a celebration of God's creative and redemptive acts. (Gen. 2:1-3; Exod. 20:8-11; 31:13-17; Lev. 23:32; Deut. 5:12-15; Isa. 56:5, 6; 58:13, 14; Ezek. 20:12, 20; Matt. 12:1-12; Mark 1:32; Luke 4:16; Heb. 4:1-11.)[20]

21. Stewardship

We are God's stewards, entrusted by Him with time and opportunities, abilities and possessions, and the blessings of the earth and its resources. We are responsible to Him for their proper use. We acknowledge God's ownership by faithful service to Him and our fellow human beings and by returning tithe and giving offerings for the proclamation of His gospel and the support and growth of His church. Stewardship is a privilege given to us by God for nurture in love and the victory over selfishness and covetousness. Stewards rejoice in the blessings that come to others as a result of their faithfulness. (Gen. 1:26-28; 2:15; 1 Chron. 29:14; Haggai 1:3-11; Mal. 3:8-12; Matt. 23:23; Rom. 15:26, 27; 1 Cor. 9:9-14; 2 Cor. 8:1-15; 9:7.)[21]

22. Christian Behavior

We are called to be a godly people who think, feel, and act in harmony with biblical principles in all aspects of personal and social life. For the Spirit to recreate in us the character of our Lord we involve ourselves only in those things that will produce

Christlike purity, health, and joy in our lives. This means that our amusement and entertainment should meet the highest standards of Christian taste and beauty. While recognizing cultural differences, our dress is to be simple, modest, and neat, befitting those whose true beauty does not consist of outward adornment but in the imperishable ornament of a gentle and quiet spirit. It also means that because our bodies are the temples of the Holy Spirit, we are to care for them intelligently. Along with adequate exercise and rest, we are to adopt the most healthful diet possible and abstain from the unclean foods identified in the Scriptures. Since alcoholic beverages, tobacco, and the irresponsible use of drugs and narcotics are harmful to our bodies, we are to abstain from them as well. Instead, we are to engage in whatever brings our thoughts and bodies into the discipline of Christ, who desires our wholesomeness, joy, and goodness. (Gen. 7:2; Exod. 20:15; Lev. 11:1-47; Ps. 106:3; Rom. 12:1, 2; 1 Cor. 6:19, 20; 10:31; 2 Cor. 6:14-7:1; 10:5; Eph. 5:1-21; Phil. 2:4; 4:8; 1 Tim. 2:9, 10; Titus 2:11, 12; 1 Peter 3:1-4; 1 John 2:6; 3 John 2.)[22]

23. Marriage and the Family

Marriage was divinely established in Eden and affirmed by Jesus to be a lifelong union between a man and a woman in loving companionship. For the Christian a marriage commitment is to God as well as to the spouse, and should be entered into only between a man and a woman who share a common faith. Mutual love, honor, respect, and responsibility are the fabric of this relationship, which is to reflect the love, sanctity, closeness, and permanence of the relationship between Christ and His church. Regarding divorce, Jesus taught that the person who divorces a spouse, except for fornication, and marries another, commits adultery. Although some family relationships may fall short of the ideal, a man and a woman who fully commit themselves to each other in Christ through marriage may achieve loving unity through the guidance of the Spirit and the nurture of the church. God blesses the family and intends that its members shall assist each other toward complete maturity. Increasing family closeness is one of the earmarks of the final gospel message. Parents are to bring up their children to love and obey the Lord. By their example and their words, they are to teach them that Christ is a loving, tender, and caring guide who wants them to become members of His body, the family of God which embraces both single and married persons. (Gen. 2:18-25; Exod. 20:12; Deut. 6:5-9; Prov. 22:6; Mal. 4:5, 6; Matt. 5:31, 32; 19:3-9, 12; Mark 10:11, 12; John 2:1-11; 1 Cor. 7:7, 10, 11; 2 Cor. 6:14; Eph. 5:21-33; 6:1-4.)[23]

24. Christ's Ministry in the Heavenly Sanctuary

There is a sanctuary in heaven, the true tabernacle that the Lord set up and not humans. In it Christ ministers on our behalf, making available to believers the benefits of His atoning sacrifice offered once for all on the cross. At His ascension, He was inaugurated as our great High Priest and began His intercessory ministry, which was typified by the work of the high priest in the holy place of the earthly sanctuary. In 1844, at the end of the prophetic period of 2300 days, He entered the second and last phase of His atoning ministry, which was typified by the work of the high priest in the most holy place of the earthly sanctuary. It is a work of investigative judgment which is part of the ultimate disposition of all sin, typified by the cleansing of the ancient Hebrew sanctuary on the Day of Atonement. In that typical service the sanctuary was cleansed with the blood of animal sacrifices, but the heavenly things are purified with the perfect sacrifice of the blood of Jesus. The investigative judgment reveals to heavenly intelligences who among the dead are asleep in Christ and therefore, in Him, are deemed worthy to have part in the first resurrection. It also makes manifest who among the living are abiding in Christ, keeping the commandments of God and the faith of Jesus, and in Him, therefore, are ready for translation into His everlasting kingdom. This judgment vindicates the justice of God in saving those who believe in Jesus. It declares that those who have remained loyal to God shall receive the kingdom. The completion of this ministry of Christ will mark the close of human probation before the Second Advent. (Lev. 16; Num. 14:34; Ezek. 4:6; Dan. 7:9-27; 8:13, 14; 9:24-27; Heb. 1:3; 2:16, 17; 4:14-16; 8:1-5; 9:11-28; 10:19-22; Rev. 8:3-5; 11:19; 14:6, 7; 20:12; 14:12; 22:11, 12.)[24]

25. The Second Coming of Christ

The second coming of Christ is the blessed hope of the church, the grand climax of the gospel. The Savior's coming will be literal, personal, visible, and worldwide. When He returns, the righteous dead will be resurrected and, together with the righteous living, will be glorified and taken to heaven, but the unrighteous will die. The almost complete fulfillment of most lines of prophecy, together with the present condition of the world, indicates that Christ's coming is near. The time of that event has not been revealed, and we are therefore exhorted to be ready at all times. (Matt. 24; Mark 13; Luke 21; John 14:1-3; Acts 1:9-11; 1 Cor. 15:51-54; 1 Thess. 4:13-18; 5:1-6; 2 Thess. 1:7-10; 2:8; 2 Tim. 3:1-5; Titus 2:13; Heb. 9:28; Rev. 1:7; 14:14-20; 19:11-21.)[25]

26. Death and Resurrection

The wages of sin is death. But God, who alone is immortal, will grant eternal life to His redeemed. Until that day death is an unconscious state for all people. When Christ, who is our life, appears, the resurrected righteous and the living righteous will be glorified and caught up to meet their Lord. The second resurrection, a resurrection of the unrighteous, will take place a thousand years later. (Job 19:25-27; Ps. 146:3, 4; Eccl. 9:5, 6, 10; Dan. 12:2, 13; Isa. 25:8; John 5:28, 29; 11:11-14; Rom. 6:23; 1 Cor. 15:51-54; Col. 3:4; 1 Thess. 4:13-17; 1 Tim. 6:15; Rev. 20:1-10.)[26]

27. The Millennium and the End of Sin

The millennium is the thousand-year reign of Christ with His saints in heaven between the first and second resurrections. During this time the wicked dead will be judged; the earth will be utterly desolate, without living human inhabitants, but occupied by Satan and his angels. At its close Christ with His saints and the Holy City will descend from heaven to earth. The unrighteous dead will then be resurrected and, with Satan and his angels, will surround the city—but fire from God will consume them and cleanse the earth. The universe will thus be freed of sin and sinners forever. (Jer. 4:23-26; Ezek. 28:18, 19; Mal. 4:1; 1 Cor. 6:2, 3; Rev. 20; 21:1-5.)[27]

28. The New Earth

On the new earth, in which righteousness dwells, God will provide an eternal home for the redeemed and a perfect environment for everlasting life, love, joy, and learning in His presence. For here God Himself will dwell with His people, and suffering and death will have passed away. The great controversy will be ended, and sin will be no more. All things, animate and inanimate, will declare that God is love, and He shall reign forever. Amen. (Isa. 35; 65:17-25; Matt. 5:5; 2 Peter 3:13; Rev. 11:15; 21:1-7; 22:1-5.)[28]

---

1. *Seventh-day Adventists Believe* (Silver Spring, MD: Ministerial Association/Review and Herald®, 2018), 11.

2. *Seventh-day Adventists Believe*, 23.

3. *Seventh-day Adventists Believe*, 35.

4. *Seventh-day Adventists Believe*, 43.

5. *Seventh-day Adventists Believe*, 69.

6. *Seventh-day Adventists Believe*, 79.

7. *Seventh-day Adventists Believe*, 91.

8. *Seventh-day Adventists Believe*, 113.

9. *Seventh-day Adventists Believe*, 121.
10. *Seventh-day Adventists Believe*, 135.
11. *Seventh-day Adventists Believe*, 151.
12. *Seventh-day Adventists Believe*, 165.
13. *Seventh-day Adventists Believe*, 185.
14. *Seventh-day Adventists Believe*, 205.
15. *Seventh-day Adventists Believe*, 217.
16. *Seventh-day Adventists Believe*, 231.
17. *Seventh-day Adventists Believe*, 243.
18. *Seventh-day Adventists Believe*, 253.
19. *Seventh-day Adventists Believe*, 269.
20. *Seventh-day Adventists Believe*, 287.
21. *Seventh-day Adventists Believe*, 307.
22. *Seventh-day Adventists Believe*, 317.
23. *Seventh-day Adventists Believe*, 333.
24. *Seventh-day Adventists Believe*, 351.
25. *Seventh-day Adventists Believe*, 373.
26. *Seventh-day Adventists Believe*, 391.
27. *Seventh-day Adventists Believe*, 407.
28. *Seventh-day Adventists Believe*, 421.